life is TOUGH

I Doubt I'll Make It Out Alive

life is TOUGH

I Doubt I'll Make It Out Alive

A MOTHER'S LIFE LESSONS LEARNED THROUGH LAUGHTER

Stacy Gooch-Anderson

CFI
Springville, Utah

ISBN 13: 978-1-59955-176-0

Published by CFI, an imprint of Cedar Fort, Inc., 2373 W. 700 S., Springville, UT 84663
Distributed by Cedar Fort, Inc., www.cedarfort.com

LIBRARY OF CONGRESS CATALOGING-IN-PUBLICATION DATA
Anderson, Stacy.
  Life is tough : I doubt I'll make it out alive / Stacy Anderson.
    p. cm.
  ISBN 978-1-59955-176-0
  1. Motherhood--Humor. 2. Mothers--Humor. I. Title.

  PN6231.M68A53 2008
  818'.607--dc22

  2008041489

Cover design by Nicole Williams
Cover design © 2009 by Lyle Mortimer
Edited and typeset by Melissa J. Caldwell

Printed in the United States of America

10 9 8 7 6 5 4 3 2 1

Printed on acid-free paper

To my family,
who has made this life one heck of a ride!

Other works by Stacy Gooch-Anderson

The Santa Letters

Contents

Preface

I was at a family gathering when my sister brought up the subject of raising children. More specifically, it was noted that those who willingly choose to raise a bunch of kids might outwardly be expressing that not only do humans enjoy the right to pursue life, liberty, and happiness but also the ability to fulfill sado-masochistic tendencies as well.

This line of conversation led to one of my four brothers asking my father to rate his children, number one being the least difficult to raise to number six being the most difficult. I understandably revolted when out of the six (per my father's sixty-year-old—and in my opinion, waning—rationale) I had come in a solid fifth! I had been unfairly slotted above my younger brother, Tom, who trumped because he had the distinction of being responsible for more gray hairs on my dad's head than the other five children combined.

That old coot, I inwardly stewed, had rated my three other brothers (Rick, Devon, and Tyler), who'd made my surname a reason to call in reinforcements at the police station, all higher than me. They'd made their acquaintances with the boys in blue while pulling capers like blowing up mailboxes, terrorizing the neighbors by displaying "full moons" from the back of a truck, and climbing church steeples at one o'clock in the morning.

Granted, my sister Bethie got the top spot, but seriously, who but a complete numbskull would cause havoc when given the keys to a new Ford Probe as an unemployed junior in high school, just so she could get back and forth to drill team practice every morning? Ahhh . . . to have such a life! That, and to be fair, she was a genuinely good kid, unable to flirt with mischief, even if it promised her the world for a fleeting smile.

What really irked me though was that while my brothers were out pulling these shenanigans, I was doing time as a shut-in locked in my bedroom, grounded from TV, phone, friends, and radio. Dad had reversed my door knob after I'd been caught locking my door as a defensive measure against my brothers. I had entertained myself by learning Morse code, so I could communicate via flashlight with my best friend down the street in an effort to remain somewhat socially involved.

I mean, really, how hard can it be to raise a teenage girl who spent ten out of twelve months her sophomore year grounded? It wasn't as if I'd been squelched for major crime sprees either. I was doing time for things like leaving dirty underwear on the floor, coming home from church five minutes late, and not washing offensive suds down the bathtub drain. From my lock up record, you'd have thought I was a close rival to Attila the Hun and as unstoppable as the Terminator.

What was it that made my parents see me as an ingrate, who needed the ever-watchful eye of a parental warden while being locked in a room that had more security than Attica?

The answer lies in perspective.

From my point of view, my parents were tyrannical nay-sayers out to ruin my life and ultimately drive me into the safety of a convent. From their perspective, however, it was simply a matter of viewing the world as a rather scary place in which to raise a precious little girl. It was a world that could easily chew up and destroy their first born, who happened to be a trusting, bright-eyed, and vulnerable young lady. They wanted to keep me safe. They would've done anything to avoid having to look into my eyes one day and realize that somehow, somewhere along the line, they'd managed to fail in the awesome responsibility of protecting me.

I might have been more charitable about the situation (then again, I WAS a teenager, so maybe not) if I had bothered to look at things through my dad's eyes. If I only could have found a way to view the world through the eyes of this man who'd come from a family of five boys (all of which were born within a six year time period) and seen things from the perspective of a protective father who'd known many "lecherous young buggers" in his lifetime.

The irony of the whole situation was that after wailing about the unfairness of it all and having been shut down without even a faint glimmer of hope of changing my position on the list, my brother Rick—three years my junior—laughed and pretended to be a water skier.

"Yeah, it was great being next in line behind you, Stace. You were like the boat cutting waves, while I just hung out enjoyin' life in your wake."

Needless to say, education often changes perspective, and I was more than happy to educate my parents on the realities of growing up with rather inquisitive and adventurous brothers.

That brings me to another point—time.

Time also changes perspective. Where twenty years before, my brothers would have seen a bit more of my dad's ire and a swift kick in the pants, and I would've gotten grounded for four and half months for being a tattletale, the present day brought us all some well-deserved laughter and an enjoyable evening as we skipped down memory lane.

Education and time, they have done wonders for our family unity.

It's also a fact of life that some people just have to do things with a more hands-on approach and with uniquely characteristic flair. Such were the ways of Tom who, as I mentioned before, got the distinction of being at the very bottom of the list.

It must be said that he alone has given our family more to laugh about than any other single child or, for that matter, all of us combined. Mind you, however, that after all of his antics, it has taken close to a decade for us to finally admit that the mere thought of his extracurricular activities on any given night doesn't cause a stinging case of heartburn anymore.

You see, we now all have time, education, and perspective on our side.

Before you begin to muse about the mental state of the author behind these words, I want you to know that all of this rambling does have a point. It's why I chose to write this book.

Life has been kind to me (overly generous really) when it comes to handing me its lessons and forcing growth in all dimensions. Where once there was a young and impetuous bright-eyed youth, there is now an older impetuous sleepy-eyed hag.

Yes, I jest. I don't look sleepy-eyed if I use enough concealer to hide the bags under my eyes and get at least ten hours of sleep. All kidding aside, time, education, and gained perspective have helped me attain some valuable insights to this journey we call life.

With that being said, it is my desire to share these life's lessons with you, not in a preachy or overly deep manner, but in a simplistic and hopefully American apple pie-ish way that will help you to feel that you are not alone, allow you to gain perspective in the everyday charms of life, and give you a good dose of laughter.

I add the last ingredient because laughter is what ultimately makes all those big, ugly horse pills with names like adversity, frustration, sadness, stress, and anger a little easier to swallow. Besides, if we can't laugh at ourselves and find even small moments of comfort in the process of growth and maturity, then rest assured, the rest of the world will. And believe me, it's no fun when you're the only one excluded from the party.

One more note, per my brothers' requests, names—other than mine, Brad's, and our boys'—have been changed, in this case, to protect the guilty.

S. G. A

Acknowledgments

I have to first thank my parents, Bill and Laurel, because they are the ones who taught me the lessons that mattered. It was while capturing those lessons—earmarked with a dose of laughter—that this book came to be, as a means to help my dad through his chemo treatments. It was his wish, through many chuckles and shared moments, that I seek publication in order to help others to find the laughter in life.

It was my mom's wish to see me reach my potential.

I also have to give BIG hugs to my siblings and the rest of my extended family (who shall remain nameless to protect the guilty) since they have graciously allowed our lives to be an open book. I love you all and wouldn't be who I am today without any of you.

But mostly, I have to extend my gratitude (and, yes . . . fulfill the requirements of the bribery contracts) and absolute love to my husband, Brad, and my sons, Justin, Mitch, Josh and Maison. YOU are my life . . .

I'd also like to thank Kammi Rencher for taking a chance on me, Melissa Caldwell for being such a super editor, and the rest of the folks at Cedar Fort, whose mission it is to put out books that make a difference.

And finally, I'd like to thank all of the good doctors and nurses at Huntsman, but namely Drs. Burt, Randall, Weiss, and Scaife and nurses Emily and Maggie, who worked tirelessly to wage the war against cancer while finding the way to bless my life through your service to my mom and dad.

You *do* make a difference, and may you one day find the cure.

Life Lesson Number One:

Broaden your horizons.

Bottoms Up

My family is weird. As much as I wish it were different, there's just no getting around it. They're just simply weird. They have good hearts and everything, but even I, who is about as normal as they come, stand back viewing this bunch as an anomaly in the circle of life. I mean, aren't parents supposed to raise their offspring until the roles are reversed? You know, when the parents begin to wear diapers, forget to brush before bedtime, and have to be reminded to take their multivitamin.

So how come I had to be stuck in a family who thinks extreme recessive behavior is an admirable trait? Let's take, for example, their penchant for living in the past. I mean it's really sad when their idea of a good time is to sit around and watch old home movies on a dilapidated white screen that, at its best, will stand at a proud 36" by 48" for twenty minutes before collapsing in sheer exhaustion.

This failure to remain vertical usually happens about the time one of my brothers (the lucky one who was chosen to wedge his foot between the screen and some piece of furniture to stabilize it) gets a charley horse in the arch of his foot.

The screen "yogi" then howls and rubs his rebelling muscle into submission. Dad sputters and curses a litany of new four-letter words and throws one of his well-worn leather slippers, with years of accumulated pine gum and anti-freeze, in its general direction. Dad, who's thankfully a lousy aim, misses the screen completely and almost hits the yoga master, who's now hopping around trying to work a knot out of his muscle. Dad literally creaks as he gets up and lumbers across the room, stepping over my siblings' bodies, which litter the room's floor like a pride of lions, so he can whip the screen into full shape once again.

My mother, who has a propensity for putting feelings into inanimate objects, naturally defends it. "Don't get so angry, dear. You know, I've noticed that you're also having a hard time standing for long periods of time as you get older."

"Don't even go there." He glares at her as everyone starts to snicker.

I shake my head back and forth, realizing that this, as is the habit of this sarcastic and self-proclaimed witty bunch, is about to degrade into yet another conversational lesson on the art form of double entendre.

Dad surprises us by not taking the bait.

Instead, he flips the screen into the air, snagging it from a graceful descent, and wrangles it as if it were a calf left over from his days as a participant in the small rodeos of southern Arizona.

To and hither, up and down, side to side it goes until it's . . . futile.

He tries a different tact. He stretches it three times and then reverse wraps it, tying a few knots in the string he's enlisted to help with the efforts, and adds a few more twists in between.

Watching his labors is a déjà vu moment. Haven't I seen this before?

Then it hits me. Ringling Bros, big top, snow cones—you get the picture. Visions of a clown, a master balloon twister we'd seen at the circus, danced, or rather jiggled, before my eyes. The only differences between Dad and the painted professional was that Dad wore a smaller shoe size and his chin waddled frantically under the strain of his efforts.

He sets the screen down, retrieves the slipper, and returns to operate the projector. It's taken forty-five minutes to get to this point, where we're ready to make it through yet another fifteen to twenty minutes of film before the process starts all over again.

At least we hadn't voted to view the slides tonight. I always pass out from hyperventilation at least once when it comes time for us to encircle the projector, so we can blow into the motor that's overheated while Mom loads yet another wheel, and Dad again fights the screen. The slides aren't so bad except for the fact that Mom can never figure out how to put them right side up. You'd think that twenty years of practice would make her an expert by now. Not so. She just laughs and tells us that "memory night," as she calls these debacles of patience, would not be quite the same without a kink in the neck that lasts through the millennium.

Mom then casually pulls out a blue reel about the size of a lid on a family-sized Smuckers grape jelly jar. "Oh look! It's our favorite movie!"

I sigh and once again lament my life amongst this band of goons. "Do we really have to?"

"Absolutely!" My father chortles and chokes on the phlegm he's coughed up. He snickers at the mere thought of once again feasting upon this captured moment in time.

"We've watched that thing so many times already, it's a wonder the film hasn't snapped from overuse."

"Oooh, but it has," coyly replies my mother. "We made enough copies to last us a lifetime, though," she coos as she pulls out a shoe box filled with at least seventy of those darn little reels all labeled "The Backyard Pool."

I slouch back into the overstuffed couch with my lips pursed and arms folded across my chest. I grimace and bore my eyes into the souls of anyone who cares enough to want to know how I feel about this mutiny.

No one does.

My brothers roll around, romping in a mock war of super studs, while Dad prepares the reel, and Mom sits by, organizing her stockpile of the most embarrassing moment of my life. I will know that I have met "Mister Right" when I can look into his eyes after seeing this movie and find compassion for what I've been made to sit through all these years.

If he laughs, he is so out the door.

With a grand flair, my father twirls his hands above his head in a beckoning gesture and announces, "It's show time!" I resist the impulse to yank out the hair that is still left on the top of his head, especially that little tuft he back combs to give him "height."

Rick, having gotten the cramp out of his foot, runs to turn off the light. Devon then takes his turn, positioning his foot between the screen and the hutch, and settles back into his contorted position. Mom snuggles between Bethie, "Kitty" (a stuffed vampire-ish looking dog with black ears, fangs hanging out of its mouth and a pink yarn bow attached to its forehead), and Tyler, who's dressed in yellow ducky pajamas that are three sizes too big. Tommy tries to be inconspicuous as he sits behind the large palm in the corner, waiting to jump out at the most appropriate time to become a human pointer when everyone laughs at the antics on the screen.

The machine clicks away in a frenzy, bringing the still images to life. Darkness precedes the little girl on the screen, who is wearing a splashy neon colored two-piece bathing suit with rolls of flesh hanging over the side of her britches, waving happily to the camera. If only she had known then that her babyish fat rolls, cheeky grin, and innocent childish antics would forever be held up as a form of public humiliation and used as a catalyst for laugh-until-you-wet-yourself laughter.

The little blue-eyed, blonde, and pasty cherub then makes a mad dash to the backyard pool. A note must be made here that every family in Arizona, or so it seemed, had a pool. They came in different shapes, hues of blue, and sizes. Ours just happened to be in the shape of a sea shell and was about 9 inches deep and three feet in diameter. That, unfortunately, didn't matter one iota to the bathing beauty on the dilapidated screen. She does a beautiful worm dive: a combination swan dive and starting gun platform push-off, used by real swimmers at the beginning of a race.

She cheerfully wallows around, circling a medley of tub toys and swimming with her bottom flapping in the wind, which looks like a grossly maimed shark fin with a crack forming down the middle.

This is Tom's cue.

He jumps into the picture and points to my posterior and then proceeds to pantomime a Great White shark, circling a yellow rubber ducky. Everyone hoots and swipes at the droplets being siphoned from the corners of their eyes.

"I hate this movie!" I snap, and then resume my pouting.

"Why?" asks my father with feigned surprise. "It's not like you're the butt of this family's jokes." Everyone roars with laughter, which encourages my father to engage the reverse button about fifty times for emphasis.

"Stop it already! I know I look ridiculous, but I thought one was supposed to be comfortable within the confines of a family. Do you have any idea how you all have disappointed that little girl," I mournfully say while pointing to the screen that has miraculously managed to stay up during this whole degrading episode.

"You were twelve years old," snickers my second brother.

"Thirteen, but that's beside the point. Security is what's it's all about."

"You mean 'a butt'?" gasps Dad in-between guffaws.

After the laughter dies down, my mother says, "We'd better move along now or we'll get a bit 'behind.' " She giggles as I eyeball her through the darkness.

"Well then, bottoms up!" Rick holds his glass of milk in toasting position and chugs the rest of it before belching and wiping his mouth on his sleeve.

I throw a cookie at him and mull over the image on the screen.

It is then that the revelation of life's first big lesson comes to me in the form of a picture of a little girl (okay, a teenager), swimming around in a cramped little pool.

It is time to broaden my horizons.

Life Lesson Number Two:

✎

It's all about the journey,
not the quickness of pace.

Watch for Those Warning Signs

Having grown up in places such as Arizona, California, and Missouri, I never got much opportunity to ski. Heck, I didn't even know what the word meant. In Utah (my eleventh home in fifteen years), however, you couldn't live on the East benches unless you knew how to ski or snowboard without being subjected to a thrashing that made a heavy-weight prize fight look like a dispute between two choir boys.

This lack of knowledge combined with aspirations to continually broaden my horizons was the impetus which led me to accept an invitation to spend the day at one of Utah's finest ski resorts.

That and naive faith.

I went with a group who I knew could teach me the finer nuances of this favorite past time—this Rocky Mountain passion or Wasatch death wish, depending on how you looked at it. Donny, Lee, and Jason were certified ski bums who happened to take a few hours out of each day to attend classes at the local high school. They lived in parkas and goggles on the weekends and looked like burnt raccoons during the week.

To the untrained snow sport enthusiast, it's a rather curious experience to watch avid skiers as they descend the backside of a mountain. As one watches the sheer joy on those beet-red, wind-chapped faces, it's obvious that they view their sport as something akin to an activity somewhere between holy rapture and a good night out. Either way, the glow from their eyes alone is enough to get you to pull out the SPF 45 sunscreen with zinc oxide and paint your nose.

My cohorts were positively giddy on the bus ride up while I was discreetly gasping for air as the atmospheric oxygen levels slowly depleted because of the ungodly high elevation. Only someone like Zeus could expect to survive in these conditions. I just prayed I wouldn't get a nose bleed. Red on white fuzzy mittens would contrast terribly with my new turquoise ski jacket.

Pulling up to the lodge, we disembarked and moved to the side of the bus where a rack held our skis. "Is this normal?" I asked Donny and gestured at the horizontal icicles clinging for life to the edges of my skis.

"Wha'da mean?" He casually looked in my direction after callously slicing a close knit group of tiny ice cilia off of his. "The ice? Yeah, it's normal, especially after post salting run-off. The water splashes up and then freezes in the wind chill."

"I see. So what happens then up on the slope when the wind is whistling past your ears and sweat or other bodily fluids are exposed?" I sniffled very aware that my nose was beginning to resemble a small dam in the last stages of structural failure.

"Let me give you a word of advice. Don't spit into the wind or you'll put out an eye or chip a tooth. Just kiddin', Stace. It just freezes to your face." I stared at him in horror as he removed his skis from the rack and jaunted off. I looked at this white land devoid of citrus trees and wished I was back in Arizona.

After chipping off more than half the ice from my skis, I took a step back from the bus so I could pull frozen shards out of my mitten tips. That's when a slight movement from the corner of my eye caught my attention. I turned just in time to catch my pair of ice-free skis across the bridge of my nose. If the lack of oxygen hadn't made me feel dizzy, then the quick swelling of my nose, cutting off my air flow, most certainly did! Vanity quickly overcame me as I pulled my goggles down hoping to hide a beak that was turning a most unbecoming shade of purplish-black and blue

I scraped the frost off one of the bus windows so I could look at my reflection and adjust my eyewear before pulling my floppy hat down a little lower and tightening the strap on my goggles. It was no use. There was no way to completely hide the misfortune of ill luck while still keeping a "coolness" quotient intact. I sighed, realizing that there was no possible way to be suave as I looked at the bus window through amber colored lenses. All delusions aside, I felt and looked like a fly.

I bent to retrieve my skis before jabbing them into the snow like I'd seen everyone else do. I must've hit an ice spot because they wouldn't sink far enough to stand on their own. I moved over and poked again. No go. Three more steps, same result. "So," I thought to myself, "maybe I'm standing on an iceberg hidden by a dusting of powder. Either way, I'm certainly not going to be beaten by something I can eliminate with a blow torch or a bucket of hot water."

I started forcefully jamming the ground with the butt end of my skis like a jackhammer operator, when Donny, sensing my frustration, offered some advice.

"Maybe if you take your gloves off and remove the poles from your wrist. They're kinda preventing the skis from going in very far. Oh, and come over here where there isn't pavement under the snow pack."

"I knew that."

"Sure you did." He laughed as he patted me on the back and went to put on his boots.

I took off my gloves, removed the poles, walked over to the rest of the group, and firmly thrust my skis into the ground. I would have stepped back at this point, but I had yet another small snag in this thoroughly enjoyable experience—my hands were securely frozen to the infernal things.

My skis had seemingly been put into a deep freeze by the

twenty-three below wind chill factor while riding outside the bus. Meanwhile, I had been sweating my butt off inside along with 219 of my closest friends in their colorful winter attire. We looked like a convention of Michelin men bound for Mardi gras, but I digress. Apparently, a chemical reaction happens when extreme cold is introduced to extreme or even moderate heat. It's called superglue.

In maneuvers that must have looked like I was waltzing with my skis, I nodded greetings to passersby. I intermittently spit onto the contact points where my hands were fused. After several minutes of frenzied spinning, spitting, and salutatories to three-fourths of the human life up on the mountain, I was able to detach my limbs and forge onward to the next step—putting on my boots.

That went pretty smoothly, until I tried to move.

Evolution had dictated since the days of cavemen that a man's stance become more and more erect. That was of course until some dolt with a fondness for waxed boards and steep hills came along and decided to upset the whole process. A whole lifetime of walking erectly with my hips in alignment went out the window. I was forced by neon blue hard plastic boots, which looked like elephant feet, to either dislocate my hips or walk like an ape with my knuckles dragging on the ground.

"You havin' a hard time with those boots, Stace?" Lee smiled.

"They aren't boots. They're unnaturally formed ankle casts." He laughed and walked as easily as a two dollar hooker in stilettos while I clomped along behind him heading for our skis.

I clipped myself rather painlessly into the bindings (a rather apropos name for something that keeps one attached to skids that zing you down a mountain) and after a few lessons on how to move on greased boards the size and width of a ten foot door jam, seated myself on the chair lift. Mind you—the chair lift is a suspended bench that swoops the rider 150 feet into the air onto a cable via an unstable-looking little wheel and a "j" hook, teetering without a harness or even a seat belt. Not a good spot to be in if you're afraid of heights.

I dealt with it though.

I harnessed every bit of mental toughness I possessed by performing simple mind over matter tricks, like focusing on focal points and deep breathing. Who was I kidding? Besides getting the attention of anyone within a one hundred yard radius with deep agonizing breaths interlaced with moans, I only managed to succumb to terror and make Jason, the mellowest out of my three ski buddies, think I was going into labor.

"Breathe, Stace. Breathe and relax."

"I am breathing, you idiot! If I breathe any deeper I'm gonna pass out from hyperventilation and fall to my death."

"My, aren't we snippy?" I glared at him in between breaths. "Okay, okay, focus on the happy little people down there swishing down the mountain having a good time."

"You're kidding right?"

"No, why?"

"If I look down it will only remind me of how freakin' far up I am on this flippin' thing! I could easily see myself falling and becoming an inconvenient speed bump for a few dozen of those happy little nuts swishing down the mountain!"

"Good point. Well, then, focus on the trees right before the peak."

"Those twigs up there that look like poor quality toothpicks?"

"Exactly! You've been on this ride only thirty seconds and we've got about eight and a half minutes to go. We'll get off when you can count the needles on their branches and see exactly how many abandoned bird nests there are."

He should have told me to focus on the sign with the big black letters that read "KEEP TIPS OF SKIS UP." It normally wouldn't have been too hard to miss since it was clearly posted on the back of the lift operator's shed, which is just to the left of the skiers exit ramp. You know, the ramp. The artificial little cliff that's built up to meet your feet? Yeah, that one.

It's a deceptive little bugger that at first looks like a giant non-threatening cheese wedge but quickly morphs into a bunny hill with attitude and a thirst for beginning skiers. It crescendos up to meet your feet, leveling out to a flat top that goes on for about three feet before dropping you. You're not sure who you feel more betrayed by, the chairlift you clung for life with or that 90 degree slope that deposits you on your posterior after the nerve racking ride.

Let me expound. That three foot flat stretch is not the place to be idle or stall in an attempt to gather your bearings because whether you want to or not, you're going to get pushed down the mini-cliff by the chairlift. It shovels you out of the way before smacking you up the back of the head and then merrily heads around the corner and back on down the hill.

I had been so focused on counting the empty nests that I never read the sign. Instead I had been subconsciously swinging my anxious feet, which was what got me unceremoniously flipped from my chair headfirst into the backside of the exit slope.

After Jason, the lift operator who was nice enough to temporarily turn off the lift, and half of Utah watched as I dragged myself up to the flat surface, being bolstered by an accompaniment of applause, the lift roared back to life and the chairs began to move again. I was feeling a bit like Sylvester Stallone on top of the Russian peak in *Rocky IV*, when an older gentleman nudged me in the backside and sent me flailing down the rest of the way. At least he was nice enough to wave as he skied by. I took a much needed rest, supine in the snow with as much of my body surface clinging to stable ground as possible.

I watched my chair hover above my head in mock concern before floating off into the distance. To this day, I swear I could hear faint laughter and snickering as the empty seat bounced and swayed along the cable, heading back down the mountain in tune to its own chortles. Baptism by snow to the innocents, I'm sure it was thinking.

The ride down was fine. Fast, but fine. Except for that one small, itty-bitty part where I lost my balance and ended up sitting on my skis because weak knees and cement-like boots didn't allow me the luxury of standing up like a human being. I must admit, however, that I did learn a few lessons in physics and aerodynamics that day.

The reduced wind resistance allowed me to barrel down the slope like a flashy blue bowling ball, indiscriminately striking ski patrons and leaving a wake of destruction and flailing bodies.

I managed to fling myself into a rolling heap before cataclysmically colliding with the lift waiting line at the bottom of the hill. As I lay on my back once again, who should appear but my friend the gentleman nudger. Seeing my prone position, he came in for a landing with a perfect sideways stop giving me a mouthful of tromped upon powder. He leaned over, peering into my eyes, and imparted another one of life's lessons.

"You know, young lady, you should slow down and enjoy things a bit more. It's not about how fast you can go but about the journey itself. Take time to enjoy the ride."

"Thanks. I'll try to remember that." I mockingly grimaced as I watched him effortlessly glide to the back of the line. "Maybe I should take his advice," I muttered, looking off into the opposite direction of the lift line. I got up, brushed myself off, retrieved my skis, and happily headed over to the kiddy tow lines and inner tubes.

Life Lesson Number Three:

⟨§⚜§⟩

Seek diligently and you shall eventually find.

What D'ya Wanna Be?

What do you want to be when you grow up? The question made my head hurt. I knew there was something out there for me. There just had to be a call or a profession that would utilize all of my talents and abilities and raise me to the pinnacle of earthly existence while allowing me to cast my hand upon the face of humanity and add my monument to the world.

The problem was that I, as of yet, still wasn't sure that the two notions were necessarily simultaneous—being and growing up that is. But about the time SATs hit my junior year, and my school's career guidance counselor placed me in the number one slot on her ten most wanted list, I decided that I'd better figure out what I wanted to be for the rest of my life. As evidenced by anyone who knows me well, I am STILL debating the grow up part.

I began to watch every professional out there with a keen interest and an analytical curiosity, which drove most of them nuts. I asked my dentist what he most enjoyed about probing around in people's mouths.

"Hey, doc, is prayer a part of your daily ritual? It'd sure be a part of mine. I'd worry every day about tainted blood infecting me with that new crazy cell abscessing, lung collapsing disease from Uganda that's been goin' around. And as a matter of curiosity, just what is the best part of your job anyway?"

Maybe it was the fact that I accidentally bit him while his knuckle was under my molar that caused him to say with a mischievous glint in his eye, "Drilling—the best is drilling." And as he asked the hygienist for a roll of gauze to control the bleeding where I'd taken a chunk out of his hand, I thought I heard him say under his breath, "Without Novocain."

My mother suggested I be a lawyer. I was really good at interrogating, debating, putting people on the spot, and reducing them to tears. "Why, honey, you do it to me all the time," she said. I would've thought of that as a compliment, but most teenagers have the exact same talents.

I thought about nursing and even volunteered as a candy-striper at our local hospital. I enjoyed making people comfortable and helping them out. Then I was sent to the geriatric ward where the old people had more fun than a two-year-old with a black permanent marker in a stark white house. I thought I had a sense of humor, but these people took the cake.

I was on my rounds the first day when I met Mr. Stumpy (remember, names have been changed to protect the guilty). He was a kind, older gentleman with the barest tuft of white fuzz on his freckled head. He asked me about my family and told me about his. He shared his life's stories and allowed me to become the benefactor of his most precious secrets and proudest moments. We bonded. He even confided in me, sharing the story of Rascal, his beloved childhood dog, who had saved him from drowning under broken ice in the pond on his family's Montana farmstead. His hero, he sniffled, had later died from pneumonia.

He then brought out his pictures, carefully going through every one. I began to feel as if I were one of the loved and the cherished, a member of his family, a true part of his inner sanctum. Then, misty-eyed, he snapped out of his reverie and mentioned that his feet were cold. "Sweetie, would you mind grabbing my slippers from under the bed for me?"

"Of course," I said. How could I deny such a simple request from this sweet old man, whom I'd so readily adopted into my heart. I reached under the bed to grab . . . a LEG? I bumped my head and fell back onto my keester as Mr. Stumpy threw up his hands, kicking his femoral stub while rolling back and forth in unruly laughter. From under the bed sheets, he then extricated the rolled up blankets he'd used as a leggy decoy.

I looked back under the bed to make sure my hands had not deceived me. I gaped at the ugliest prosthesis I'd ever seen. It was the same gray pallor as Stumpy's other extremities and even sported a plush velour slipper upon what appeared to be a bony foot.

"I always love the look of disgust on you pretty gullible yung'uns faces when you meet 'ole stumpy.' "

I got up and brushed myself off while mumbling, "Is that pretty gullible as in good-looking but foolish or denser than the hair on that ugly leg?"

He laughed even harder while pantomiming the act of reeling in a big one. That's when I noticed that the picture of Rascal was actually an insert from a new Kmart picture frame. Disappointment pierced me, and I felt like the mutt had died all over again.

Then there was Geronimo. I walked into his room still believing that Stumpy was a fluke. He smiled a seductive grin and said, "Ah, my willowy Indian bride. I knew you wouldn't abandon me."

I looked over my shoulder and realizing that no one was there, instinctively turned my wrist and pointed squarely at my own chest while feigning a weak smile. "Me?"

I figured he had fairly lost it as I caught my reflection and consciously realized that I looked more like a fair complected version of a brawny Brunhilda. I saw my Swedish ancestry, but he apparently saw Sacagawea.

"Come to me, my love," he said as he snatched my wrist and yanked me to the bedside. Poor guy. I figured it wouldn't hurt to play along. "I want to show you my battle wounds." He then yelled, "Geronimo!" and ripped up his flimsy hospital gown revealing a scar that went from his shoulder down to his inner thigh.

16

The nurse walked in as I was struggling with Crazy Gown and began to chuckle. "Saw more than you expected today?"

"I guess so. When did they start performing lobotomies through the abdominal region?" She hooted and I left. Permanently.

A doctor of psychiatry was out. I'd spent enough time with one after my experiences with Stumpy and Geronimo to know that I'd rather be the weight holding the couch down than be the shrink.

I thought about being a professional athlete, but after knee surgery, my physical therapist told me that wouldn't be such a good idea when I screamed for him to make the pain go away as his hand hovered *above* my leg.

Plants (even the silk variety) died under my tutelage, so horticulture was out.

I thought leisure and travel might be a nice career, so I volunteered to plan and execute our next family vacation. I had them all excited about Paris—sandy beaches, historical landmarks, and beautiful countrysides—until we actually drove to our destination. I'm not sure why, but Mom was less than enthused. She had kicked the rancid grass from the tip of her toe while tossing her lounge chair between two boulders on the thirteen square feet of sand that constituted all of the beach space cleared of recyclable goods in Paris, Idaho.

Dad tried to be a bit more helpful by acknowledging that the Budget Nite Motel we were booked at had less cockroaches than the one he'd stayed at when all the decent rooms were taken during his last convention in Chicago.

"But, Dad, didn't you run away from that one when the roaches and mosquitoes combined forces and tried to eat you out of their home? You gave new meaning to the term fast food after that one," my brother helpfully pointed out.

"Oh, that was the one, wasn't it? This one serves much better biscuits and gravy, though. The gravy has flavor and lumps that you can identify." A travel agency career apparently was out unless I wanted to book dream vacations for rednecks.

My father forbade me to be a CPA when for the eleventh month in a row, I miscalculated the balance in my checkbook by a mere hundred or two.

I was lamenting my troubles while I looked for my cocker spaniel, Bandit. I caught him leaping like a gazelle off the single stair into my mother's living room, spraying urine all over her white rug before wiping his feet and exiting. "It's been nine months, you cretinous little hairball. Why don't you at least go on the brown carpet where we could hide it?"

My brother's voice sailed from around the corner. "Looks like animal training is out."

I started to get shaky on being an author when my creative writing teacher told me that Ernest Hemmingway had more ability to write humor while in the throes of depression than I would if I was chained to a typewriter for ninety-seven years with Erma Bombeck.

Friday night came and I was exhausted. I was quite certain that I would never grow into a responsible adult who could ever manage to do without an emergency room or a fire extinguisher nearby. But how I so desperately wanted to be something—a somebody who was good at her job!

My friends took me to the circus in a futile effort to cheer me up. I watched the three rings with little people doing physically impossible stunts. The animals were making messes while a poor slovenly clown followed demurely behind with a broom and dust pan. Best of all was the Master of Ceremonies who stood in the middle of it all with pomp and ego taking credit for all the hoopla even though he didn't do anything remotely dangerous or that which caused any exertion whatsoever.

I heard the clanging, clattering, shrieks, and screams. I smelled the burnt popcorn and smoke from the firecrackers that some mischievous midgets had set off behind two old ladies four rows down, just for the perverse joy of seeing them come unglued.

I gazed through the smoke wafting from behind their seats and recognized a spark of familiarity. It was as if a memory from long ago was lapping at the recesses of my mind. One can find answers in the most unusual ways I thought. I touched my shoes to the sticky floor with nineteen days of melted snow cones, ice cream, soda pop and cotton candy and felt the well-spring of realization continuing to bubble. I knew what I wanted to be! What I would aspire to do with my life! My career of choice!

I wanted to be a mom.

Life Lesson Number Four:

゚(ѣ♣ҙ)゚

Mastery is a line upon line,
precept upon precept concept, and even then,
there is yet another horizon to be traversed.

Biscuits Beware

A wife, a mother! The most noble and selfless of all beings! Yes, this is what I wanted to be in life. I envisioned my bright, witty, adorable children with straight white teeth dressed in insignia laden designer brands, thanking the one who made their blissfully wonderful and charmed lives possible—*me*, their sweet and estimable mother!

Take note, won't you, that their songs of praise came in the form of accolades during acceptance speeches for awards, positions, and with every conceivability, a Nobel Prize, because these children were stellar in every way!

That's when a midget clown with a bulbous, red, squeaky nose dumped a bucket full of confetti over my head, bringing me out of my serendipitous daze. As I was pulling a renegade floral dicot out of my armpit, I noticed that the clown had a heart tattooed right under the edge of his Popeye sailor shirt with the letters M-O-M printed in a barbed wire motif across the top.

I guess flattery comes in all forms.

I set out to learn all the nuances of being a good mom. It would take work—real hard work—and plenty of sponges and pine cleaner.

My mother was euphoric that I had decided to follow in her steps. She took full advantage of my desire to learn and came up with a list as long as an Alaskan winter night and also signed temporary custody of my siblings over to me. This happened before I got up the next morning for school.

I began to wonder if something was wrong when her alarm never went off. I definitely knew something was abreast when my five-year-old brother asked me what was for breakfast.

"I dunno. Go ask Mom," I groggily grumbled.

"She said ask you, you're the mom in training." I was *wide* awake now.

"*Mom!* What's he talkin' about?"

"I believe something having to do with hunger pains and breakfast. You know, you really should get to know your charges better. But I'll give you a hint . . . he likes the cocoa puffy rice." She rolled over and pulled her blankets up to her chin smacking her lips into a peaceful sleepy gurgle. I shook her until her sponge curler clips were popping from the inertia.

"I have school," I said.

"Get up earlier."

"But Mom, they're your kids."

"I'll loan 'em to you."

I sighed, folded my arms across my chest, and rolled my eyes before realizing that my display of impatience was wasted in the dark, so I changed tack.

I matter-of-factly stated, "I want to learn how to be a good mom and raise good kids."

"I won't take offense to that comment. I'll just remember that you're a product of my inferior skills."

"Eh?" I had the feeling I was losing this battle.

"Sweetheart, there is no better time than the present to try this out and decide this is really what you want to be *before* you end up punishing some sweet little thing. It's a hard job that takes a lot of skills and patience."

"I have skills," I half-convincingly said.

"I know, but we're talking about the kind that won't end you up in a court room."

"Defense or prosecution?"

"I was thinking more on the defendant side of things," she said.

"I have patience."

"That's a joke, right?" She snorted and rolled over denoting that the conversation was over.

I'd show her! I went to fill up a bowl of cocoa puffy rice. "What are you staring at, you little toad?"

"I thought that was my bowl of puffy rice," my brother said.

"Not quite, get your own."

"I'm too little."

"Get a step stool," I grumbled.

"MOOOMMMMM."

"Okay, okay, squirt, just be quiet, I'll get you your puffy rice."

Twenty-five minutes later after having gone through too much milk—a momentary lapse of judgment when it came to picking the blue bowl instead of the red one and fighting over how soggy puffy rice should get before being eaten—I still was not ready for school, and my brother was now dumping the whole bowl down the sink saying his tummy didn't feel like puffy rice, it wanted chocolate pudding.

I explained in a rather loud voice for 6:45 in the morning that I could care less if he was the King of Cairo, Hades could freeze over before I'd waste another moment making chocolate pudding for him.

That's when she walked in. My tormentor, the woman formally known as my mother. "I knew that patience bit was a gag."

"That little twerp is impossible! I'm late for school, my hair is a mess and I have a million things to do! I'll never get it all done!" I felt like crying.

"Now you're getting the hang of motherhood," she said with a coy smile. "Oh and by the way, the 'little twerp' wet his sheets again but you're in luck, it's Saturday. Plenty of time to get it all done," and with that, she handed me the list before disappearing into her cocoon of warmth and falling into the most decadently blissful sleep a person can have—that which comes when you can actually sleep in on a Saturday morning.

A few hours later he showed up at the side of my bed declaring he'd eaten too much chocolate pudding and his tummy was now mad. He wanted to crawl into bed with me. I barely had enough time to throw off all my top covers, exposing my clean white night-gown and pale coral sheets, when he explosively upchucked three gallons of curdled sour smelling chocolate pudding. He looked at the mess and then turned heading for the door.

"Hey, don't you want to sleep here?" I said as I caught the drip-ping remnants from my hair.

"Naw, your bed's yucky." He then disappeared before I could strangle him with a chocolate and coral marbleized pillowcase.

I ranted as I ripped the contoured sheet off my bed and wrapped it with the spoiled flat into a compact sheet burrito, before heading to the laundry room.

I survived the weekend. Barely.

I figured that if I was going to run the motherhood marathon, I needed some formal training. I signed up for home economics.

I sat through the first day becoming genuinely excited over the curriculum. I would learn how to bake, make gravy without lumps, sew, crochet, learn how to manage and budget money, and even become skilled in the responsibilities necessary for caring for chil-dren. (It was actually a five-pound bag of sugar with yarn hair and google eyes wrapped in a blanket, but that's beside the point.)

I became really enthused when I passed my first assignment which was making Jell-O. We moved on up the ladder of domestic-ity when we tackled such projects as macaroni and cheese, toast, and poached eggs. I was elated until "mmm . . . possible cheesecake" day. I think it was the singed eyebrows that gave me away.

My teacher strolled on over to see how I was doing and asked if I had completed my assignment. I mumbled, "Maybe," and kept my head low and my back towards her.

"Please face me when you speak. You might give me a complex."

Her gentle smile turned into a look of utter disbelief and then raucous laughter as she stuttered, "What . . . what . . . what on Earth happened to your eyebrows?"

The whole class turned to gape at the browless wonder and hear my explanation.

"Well, I spilled the almond extract, so I wiped it up. Then my forehead itched, so I scratched it and probably got the extract on my eyebrows, and then I must've gotten too close to the gas burner as I turned it on and . . . dang it Mrs. Otteran, you should tell us that stuff is flammable!"

She snickered some more. Then she said, "Well, class, you have now learned a good lesson in kitchen safety. Flammables and flame don't mix unless you're prepared to deal with the consequences." She chuckled at me and walked away.

I took my recipe card and put an *I* in front of the "mmm . . . possible" before dumping the whole pie plate into the garbage.

Sewing wasn't much better. I learned after the fact that one shouldn't start out with plaids and that patching is a lesson in futility. Nonetheless, I trudged on and then gave up only after I tried putting a button fly on the front of a golf shirt. It came out looking like my sewing machine foot had a bad case of road rage. I did salvage enough material from the back panel to make a really great napkin though. That should count for at least a few points towards the unit lesson entitled "Frugality: Wasting Not, Wanting Not." My children might go topless but at least they'd have the necessities for impeccable table manners.

Crocheting got a little better and I ended up with a queen sized fuzzy yarn bedspread with pom-poms in a nice shade of passion flower purple. I proudly presented it to Mom and Dad for Christmas. It was a little bigger than the baby blanket or scarf I was supposed to do, but I was still trying to overcompensate for the cheesecake caper. Matter of fact, they used it as a mattress cover, but that's only because Mom said the pom-poms had a nice massaging effect to them.

I did learn how to balance a checkbook to the nearest twenty.

Finally came the unit on child rearing. I excelled! I found baby-sitters for Sugar. I fed Sugar. I dressed Sugar and I even rocked Sugar. Then on the last day of the unit, I dropped Sugar. We had a quick service in class and then made sugar cookies.

Smacking my lips and licking my fingers, I noted to myself that every grandma I had ever known also had a tub full of sugar cookies. I was catching the vision here. When the kids grow beyond the cute five pound bag, you upgrade to the ten or twenty pounders that are too hard to handle and drop them off at Grandma's. Let her make something sweet out of them. So that's the secret to motherhood. Pass it off until age makes you more capable. Maybe by the time I reached grandmahood, I'd be able to handle the bigger bags too and excel in that role.

Despite what seemed like continuous failure, more than a few years after high school graduation, I found a man willing to take a chance on me (with the extended warranty my father threw in), and we married.

Soon after the honeymoon, I was trying to prove that he had not gotten the short end of the stick by proving my domestic ways. He was impressed when he saw the delicious looking golden biscuits I had made with the accompanying side of lumpless honey butter. The delight shone radiantly on his face as he went to pick one up. In less than a nano second it disappeared. Not because he was able to eat it, but because it disappeared into thin air (I happened to remember that I'd forgotten to add the milk). He looked at the residual powder left in the pan and then looked at me with caustic surprise.

"Needs a few more years of practice, hon. I'd stick with the poached eggs and macaroni and cheese for now."

Fortunately, he's given me at least a few decades to practice.

Life Lesson Number Five:

For everything truly horrible under the sun, there is, most of the time anyway, an exact and equal opposite.

Calling All Prince Charmings

Whoever publicized the theory that you have to kiss a lot of toads in order to find Prince Charming really knew her stuff! I grew up believing that karma or destiny enforced love and predicted the matches that were to be made in heaven. Little did I know that karma had as much to do with it as it did with who got the job of being the dog's pooper scooper every week. Purely and simply, it came down to a process of elimination. Well, that and who could stomach my cooking.

I spent many a disastrous Friday night on the phone crying to my best friend, Heather.

"So Stace, how did this one go?"

"It was about as enjoyable as sleeping . . . uh . . . I mean, sitting through Dr. Fernwood's mandatory three-hour biology lecture on 'The Amazing World and Multiplicity of Amoebas.' "

"That exciting, huh?"

"Excruciatingly so."

"Well, at least he wasn't Miguel."

"Aye-yi-yi. Don't remind me of that one! I seriously thought I was going to need a hip replacement after trying to keep up with his Latin gyrations. Fortunately it was just a dislocated tailbone. That pillow ring I had to pack around came in handy though when I clobbered Sylvester for taking me to that Jell-O Wrestling Showdown as an unauthorized contestant. You know, I think it would be much easier if we could just shop for Mr. Right like you do for a hamburger at McDonalds. I'll take one Mr. Dark-n-handsome with the tight buns and top him off with intelligence, wit, compassion, and a little adventurousness. Oh, and hold the acne and supersize the muscles. Throw in a side of apple-pie Americana charm, and I'll take him to go!"

"Hmmm, wouldn't that be the life? Maybe next weekend will be better."

"Oh, it will, it will."

"How come you sound so sure?"

"Because Reginald asked me out."

"You can't be serious! He has mambo lips with the suction power of the newest Hoover and an ego bigger than the dam by the same name! Tell me you're kidding!"

"Now don't go gettin' your nerve cells on an anxiety bender! I told him I was busy. It's perm and frost night with my mom."

"Is that true?"

"Absolutely! We planned it after I got off the phone with him. It should take us about an hour and a half if we start promptly at four. I'll call you after we're done, and we'll go out for sorbet."

I never called her.

Reginald showed up on a lark, just in case I got done early and still wanted to go. The plastic hood with bits of pulled-through hair, swimming in bleach solution and the acrid smell of perm burning his nose, didn't even dissuade him.

Mom was no help.

She looked at that lip (which I might add reminded me of an orangutan named Fester I'd met on my last date to the zoo), gave me a wickedly devilish smile, and said, "Why, Reginald, we'll be done in about ten minutes. Have a seat in the living room." He turned to leave and soon after, his lip followed.

I glared at her in such a way that she knew without a doubt I would make it my mission to get even. I'd do it when she was least expecting it, when she thought the memory of this moment was forever gone! I'd do it when she was at her most vulnerable and trusting. I'd send the kids to Grandma's house the week after Halloween, when they were doped up on sugar and higher than kites!

He drove me to see *Top Gun*. I then paid for us to get in because he was six dollars short of the seven dollars it took to get into the movie. I almost smacked him when, with feigned gentlemanlikeness and a deep bow, he mentioned that he loved women with resources. I lucked out when a family of five asked if the seats next to us were taken. He got up to move to the opposite end while I stayed in the aisle seat. My godsend in the form of a mother of three asked me if I'd like to sit by my boyfriend.

"That's okay. He's not really my friend and I'm beginning to wonder if he's really a boy or an ape. I'll hook up with him after the flick." She looked in his direction, looked back at me, and nodded in understanding.

"Well, Reg, Cruise was great. Now shall we? Cruise home that is."

He insisted on pretending that his car was an F-15 fighter as he dodged in and out of traffic in sync to the song on the radio, which unfortunately happened to be *Danger Zone* by Kenny Loggins. I was so nervous that I barely noticed when his bottom lip smacked my neck as he swerved from right to left. I wasn't even really sure it had happened at all until a welt underneath a bit of misplaced drool appeared.

"You know, Reg, my curfew is 9:30 and if I'm late, I'll get grounded for ninety days or until I drive my parents nuts, whichever comes first. What time is it?"

"It's 9:42."

"Gee, Reg, that's too bad. Well, look for me next quarter. Oh, did I mention that grounding at my house means no phone, social activities, and contact from any soul living or deceased?"

I opened the door of his car ready to leap before he could come to a complete stop when *she* appeared in her fuzzy bathrobe and called from the doorway, "You kids seem like you're having a good time! You can stay out until 10:30 tonight, dear! I don't want to rain on your evening."

I swear I heard her cackle as she closed the door.

"Let's go where romance can flow!" And with that he gunned his engine as I fell back into the bucket seat, and the door slammed from the inertia like a death knell.

Five minutes and some serious slobber later (I know St. Bernards that secrete less lip juice than Reginald), I was bounding out of the car and running for cover. That lip hovering above my throat had given me an image I couldn't quite cope with. He was completely stumped as I ducked under a deck and headed for the nearest woods.

"Why are you running away?"

I stopped long enough to reply. "Reginald, when I'm with you I feel as if there's a noose around my neck, *and laws*, how I wish there was so I could end the misery and hang myself!" He looked at me blankly before laughing and placing his hands on his hips with a flair of supreme confidence.

"That was the best quip I've heard in a long time . . . How about tomorrow?"

I turned in utter disbelief and marched down the hill. "I swear it'll be a cold day in hades before I date again."

Brad flew in from the East Coast the next day, and our first date was that night.

I had been aflutter all afternoon, a fact that did not go unnoticed by my family as I sprayed Binaca in my hair and spritzed White Rain on my tongue. He was coming over to make burritos and watch a movie. I popped a bean into my mouth as my brother chided in mock sentiment, "Beans, beans, good for your heart, the more you eat the more you—"

I chased him out of the kitchen with the meat tenderizer and then unceremoniously dumped the beans into the garbage disposal. A puff of gas erupted from the unit as it whirred into action.

I think the family was astute in figuring that this one was special. As such, my dad met him at the front door and ushered him into the living room. He motioned for Brad to sit down on the couch as he took the wingback chair, which had a wing span a condor would be proud of. It was quite an imposing chair that looked like it could take off at any second and swoop in on the prey across from it, the person who, I was sure, would formerly be known as the guy in my life.

The serious old coot, twisting his bushy eyebrows into miniature spears and sitting on the lap of the chair, didn't help either. My beloved probably would've run back through the front door if he hadn't been trying to erase the image of dad in his slippers and slightly twisted sweatpants, trying to hide the gas that escaped every time he took a step as he led him into this room.

He pulled from behind him a fake gun (which would've been a good knock-off if this meeting were happening in a dark alley) and laid it ever so gently on the coffee table. He off-handedly said, "I'll shoot off every finger or appendage that touches my daughter inappropriately."

Without looking back, he noisily crinkled a magazine he'd grabbed off of the coffee table to hide his trotting problem. Padding on out of the room, Dad said, "I'll go get Stace."

I was amazed that my short blond Adonis didn't run. He obviously didn't know what was yet in store for him—the interrogation from Mom, Grandma, and Aunt Emily. They covered menial stuff like his bank account balance, lineage, past dating history, and GPA since kindergarten. They also felt it their duty to let him know of my inability to conquer anything remotely domestic, including the pot roast the previous Sunday.

"That thing was so tough," Grandma said, giggling, "that her father had to use a chain saw to cut it. We sprinkled it with soy sauce and seasonings and had beef jerky for a week. Here, I'll go get you some." She was off in a flash.

By the time their questions had all been satisfied, and we were finally alone, I had fallen sound asleep on the floor and the movie was on auto rewind. Suddenly, I jumped up, ran to the kitchen, and while whirling in circles as if to find something, said in a panicky voice, "The pot roast is burning! Now where did I put that Crock-Pot?"

With as much suddenness as the first scene, I shrugged my shoulders and returned to the floor, nestling back into slumber quite unaware of the fool I'd just made of myself.

I'm not quite sure what went through his head, after witnessing that twilight moment and chewing on pot roast jerky. Nonetheless, he tickled the back of my neck as he watched me slumber.

We were married five months later.

Life Lesson Number Six:

Sometimes it's better to leap first and then look. The view might scare you otherwise.

Little Things Come in Big Packages

If the whole dating thing was classified as unnerving, then conversing with Brad's parents post-engagement fit into a whole other realm. I'd place it equal to the panic I would've felt if I ever met a grizzly bear just out of hibernation, who saw that I was slathered with thirteen pounds of bacon spatter, without running shoes or a tree in sight. Sitting across from Brad's parents, I felt just as vulnerable too.

Don't get me wrong, they truly are delightful people. It's just that my intentions towards their son weren't as honorable anymore. I wanted him, and I wanted him all to myself without the benefit of his mother's homemade vanilla ice cream or chicken enchiladas to distract him. They had known me as the girl up the street, who was Brad's good friend, not the home wrecker who had nabbed him from the four-eyed fish face that was his sister's best friend. (She really wasn't a four-eyed fish face, but hey, exes have to be made into monsters so, as the new girl in a guy's life, we can sleep well at night.)

After our forthcoming announcement, I was pretty sure I would heretofore be known as the backstabbing hussy, who had stolen their baby boy in order to underfeed him with a steady diet of beans and weenies, macaroni and cheese, and possibly Cheerios if he needed a little fiber in his diet.

I had to seriously wonder if Brad's parents would willingly hand him over, after I'd stolen his heart and backed him into a corner of marital bliss amongst orange shag carpet (circa 1972), which needed to be raked and vacuumed twice a day so no living thing could nest in it.

Would they ever look at me as the vitamin in his diet of love, after they'd been to our basement apartment—decorated in early Salvation Army and without air conditioning or an electrical outlet in the bathroom—because that's what our budget could afford?

Could I really believe that they'd trust me to raise their grand-children in such a way that they could permanently glue their felt leaves to the decorative family tree in the front hallway without trying to hide my offspring under a branch or in the leaf piles, half-hidden by grotesquely oversized roots?

These were the thoughts racing through my mind when Brad harshly shoved an elbow up under my rib cage. "Breathe," he whispered, "and peel that stupid grin off your face. It looks unnatural, and if you should expire due to a lack of oxygen, I don't wanna chance rigor mortis freezing it that way. You look like the clown at the Jack in the Box drive-through."

He shuddered at the mere thought of it. "Besides, I haven't told them yet." The cheesy grin slid right off my face like an egg out of a Teflon pan.

"Why not? We've been engaged for three hours!"

"I haven't broken up with my girlfriend yet."

"Oh. Well, I guess that makes sense. When were you planning on getting around to that?"

"It's on my list of things to do for Monday morning."

Monday evening, Brad said grace before dinner and added the words, "And let Mom and Dad accept the fact that I'm getting married in four months . . . to Stacy."

He heard sudden, although expected, choking as he calmly

opened his eyes and placed a paper napkin on his lap. When he looked up, the olive his mother had snuck during the prayer, along with the chunk of phlegm she'd gagged on, flew across the table and hit him in the forehead. She stared at him, wiped her mouth, and then served the green beans. Nothing else was said until I met the rest of his family.

This engagement gig was wearing me out. I was trying day and night to be the perfect catch before Brad or his family got wise and discovered that there was something fishy swimming into their lives. Besides, the extended warranty my father had thrown in was up for renegotiation in ninety days.

Would I have to live like this for the rest of my life?

When would I be able to go back to my favorite wash-and-wear clothes with character wrinkles instead of the iron-every-twenty-minutes-linen slacks I'd recently acquired in an attempt to convey class and polish?

Could I ever quit scraping and putting cinnamon on his toast to hide the fact that I'd burnt it yet again?

At what point in the relationship could I yell back at having my tires kicked one too many times and rebel at his hand being possessively placed on my back as he told everyone that I was a classic beauty in an Edsel sort of way?

If they ever saw me without curled locks, matching coordinates, and full eyelashes that I had to tease, curl, and coat three hundred times until they appeared, would they ask Brad to throw me back and go for a goldfish instead of a sturgeon?

I decided to ask someone who would know, someone who'd been down this road before.

"Mooommmm! Are you home?"

"Down here, honey." I headed to the basement and found her on her back with the Mylar balloon Brad had given me for my birthday floating in circles above her.

"What are you doing down there?" I said as I grabbed the balloon and plopped down on the couch. She winced as she rolled over onto her knees and crawled over to the couch.

"That dang balloon has floated around here for the last month, drifting from around corners, down hallways, and out of closets, scaring the daylights outta me. I'd had enough, so when I saw it hovering on the floor over there, I ran and jumped on it with both feet. I thought it would pop, but it decided to flip me onto my backside and mock me from a few inches beyond my reach. Those things are a lot sturdier than a 112 pound woman."

"124, Mom. I've seen the scale."

"It's off by a few pounds. I need to adjust it. What's on your mind?

"How long before I can be my natural self and show my fiancé what I look like in the morning with a face that looks like a geisha with fourth degree acne and breath that would knock a camel over?"

"Theoretically or fact-based?"

"Both"

"Well, theoretically speaking of course, if you were the child of Christie Brinkley and Fabio, Maybelline wouldn't matter, unless of course, you wanted to knock the socks off of Jon Bon Jovi. There's something about his vocals . . ."

"That doesn't help me much."

"Neither do your genes, dear. The fact is that you're my child and your father still hasn't seen me without makeup. I go to bed with it on just in case there's a fire or he has to turn on the light to find his Rolaids. I'd hate for him to choke on one after getting a look of this mug without mascara, blush, and a touch of lip liner."

I didn't think things could get worse than staring at a future with face pores that'd never see natural light again without a layer of Ivory Mist foundation and concentrated concealing powder, but they did. It happened the day my dad received his spring edition of the Victoria's Secret catalogue and looked at it through the eyes of a father sending his daughter into the arms of a young man rather than through the perspective of a husband looking for Easter decorations for his wife to wear.

He promptly rushed to Walmart in search of the biggest,

baggiest, lacey pastel undies he could find in the granny department. He found them wedged between the Lycra support hose and double D industrial strength bras with the 11-inch wide support straps and 14 closure eye hooks. He left them on my bed.

As I stood there holding them pinched between my index fingers and thumbs, my mother peered around the doorjamb. "So, do you like them?"

"Are they windsocks for a 747?" Mom looked shocked.

"Noooo . . ."

"Then, NO! I don't like them!" I pulled a pair on over my clothes and yanked it all the way up to my chin. "Is it underwear or full body armor?"

She laughed and said, "He just wanted you to have something nice for your honeymoon."

"Are you serious? Does he ever want grandchildren? Oh, I can see it now. All I need is a ribbon attached so I can tie it around my neck and wear them as a full length teddy. Maybe I can then tantalize my husband by playing the part of an 1892 brothel dame."

I folded them down once.

"Look, if I want to look like I live in this century, I can wear them as underwear and a ruffled skirt *at the same time*. Why, if I really want to be creative, I can add a plaid shirt, hose that wrinkle at my ankles and a straw hat with a price tag, and I'd be a dead ringer for Minnie Pearl."

"They're not that bad." Mom grimaced as I exaggeratedly sashayed around in my tricot skirt. She lightened up a bit as she said, "You could use them to make curtains for your new apartment or how about sheets for the water bed?"

I flopped across my mattress. "That'd take care of the first three pairs, but what do I do with the other thirty-six?" She laughed and walked down the hall.

The next week was Brad's twenty-fourth birthday. In celebration, his mom decided to invite the whole family over so they could also officially announce our engagement. Better to only have to do it once, she said.

Now it was a well-known fact that Brad's grandfather lived for three things: his wife's Sunday pot roasts, golfing with his buddies, and most of all, fishing with his grandson. So, in order to impress the 88-year-old patriarch, I scoured the valley for a birthday card that had to do with fishing to enclose with Brad's birthday gift. I finally found one that had a picture of a man wearing a hat with numerous flies attached to the brim, sitting in an old wooden boat with a line in the water. The words above the picture read, "How do you catch a lot of fish in a very little time?"

Sounded good to me. I grabbed the card and flew to the checkout line. I was running late yet again.

When I walked into the room holding my beloved's hand, his grandmother gasped and said, "Where's the other one, you know, the one from up north? This isn't the one you're going to marry, is it?"

My future mother-in-law winced. "He broke up with her a few weeks ago, Mother. He's going to marry Stacy."

"Oh, that's a shame. I liked what's-her-name," she said as she glanced towards the picture of Brad's ex still being displayed on their bookshelf. Brad just smiled at me and inconspicuously gestured for me to tuck in my underwear.

When Grandpa came to my gift, he opened the card and read it out loud.

"How do you catch a lot of fish in a very little time?" He opened the card and read the inside. I'd been in such a hurry, I hadn't taken the time to peruse the advice.

"Go naked, and they'll come up dying of laughter."

Whoops. Aaahh, hummm, well, uhh, . . . I guess I should've taken a moment to read it before I opened myself and my sweetheart up to such humiliation. I could feel his ex's sneering smile laughing from within the photograph, while her weasel eyes bored into my back. My cheeks flushed purple with acute embarrassment. I was thinking about how much I'd love to send the ex a dozen Mylar balloons for her next birthday when Grandpa piped in.

"I knew I liked this girl. She tells it like it is and undoubtedly knows what little she's gettin'.'" He roared with laughter and slapped his knee before pounding Brad on the back. My fiancé turned a nice shade of fuchsia. Everyone else joined in, and we had a good laugh for the next half hour.

Maybe this was a family after all with whom I could afford a few allowances of trust and not be afraid to use nighttime makeup removal cream, but only on those nights I was sure there wasn't going to be a fire or that my husband didn't have acid indigestion.

Life Lesson Number Seven:

Marriage is like writing a symphony. It takes time, patience, and creativity while you build it one note at a time. And in times of utter discouragement, remember that even Beethoven, who was tone deaf, persevered to conquer the keys and create perfect harmony.

To Eternity and Beyond

Is it a bad omen when you're late to your own wedding or does it just let the groom know what to expect for the next half a century?

The alarm went off at 6:00 AM. I peeked at the glowing lime green numbers and somewhat consciously thought, "Ceremony is at 9:30. I could do my hair in twenty minutes, makeup in ten, dress in ten, and go through my checklist in twenty. Gather the AWOL items in another thirty, wait for mom and grandma to decide whether to wear suede or leather pumps—forty-five (at least). And pick one more fight with my brother *and win,* reminding him who was still queen of the pigs—fifteen minutes. Ten to polish my nails before getting into the car to blow them dry in front of the air conditioner, a half hour in travel and parking time, ten to throw the dress on, and sprint to my cue with ten minutes to spare."

Plenty of time!

I hit the snooze button and rolled over. I woke up when I heard Grandma asking my sister if she liked the suede or leather pumps.

I came stumbling out of my room with knots in my hair and slobber drizzling down my chin, trying to see through two swollen slits where I was sure my eyes used to be. Holding my hand up as a shield against fourth-degree retina burn, I groggily stammered, "Why didn't anyone wake me up?"

Mom peeked around the corner of her bedroom. "Because we have a wedding to go to. We're already late."

With that she gave Grandma her other suede shoe and told her to put it on. "I'll wear leather so we won't look alike. Besides, the toe on my suedes is too pointy. I'd end up with bunions before the day's end." She then marched off.

I ran to the bathrooms (there were four), which were being occupied by those who seemed to think that their role in this day was hugely larger than my own. I finally ended up in my closet squatting before a pocket mirror trying to untangle my hair and paint my face. That's when I heard the car back out of the driveway, and the garage close.

I did my version of the matrimony sprint out to the sidewalk with the garment bag containing my dress slung over my shoulder and my shoes, nail polish, and makeup bag clutched precariously between my fingers. I made it just in time to see our station wagon disappear around the corner.

I was still standing there, gaping, when the same station wagon pulled around the opposite corner and screeched to a halt as my dad rolled down the window and said, "I knew we forgot something besides the film."

Mom opened the back door (Grandma was in the front seat) and told me to crawl to the very back. All the other seats were taken.

"So much for drying my nails by the air conditioner," I thought as I discarded the polish into the nearest cup holder.

I finished putting on my mascara and wiped the residual off my eyeball. What was left on my upper lid, I surmised, kinda looked like liner so I left it. After three strikes of trying to keep my lipstick from wandering outside my lip lines when dad hit every bump in the road, I considered it as good as it was going to get and looked up.

"You forgot the *film*?"

40

"Yes, but dad will run in really quick and get some at the camera bar." A sloth was quicker than my father in a grocery store.

The clock said 8:52. I groaned. Twenty-two minutes and fourteen seconds later, he came out with a flat of strawberries, a couple of donuts, a carton of fresh-squeezed orange juice, and a bag of pitted prunes.

"Strawberries were on sale. They looked pretty good!" He popped one in his mouth and started to chew.

"Did you get the film, dear?" Mom asked. He quit chewing.

"I knew I forgot something." He grabbed a few more strawberries and sauntered back into the store.

We made it downtown faster than a dragster doing a quarter mile. One must understand that when driving with my father, there are a few rules he abides by. Not many of them are legal, but he abides by a few anyway:

1. A yellow light means go faster even if the hues are turning a bit rosy.
2. Change lanes first and then signal as a polite gesture to say thanks for letting me butt in.
3. And my personal favorite—"My car's bigger, they'll get out of the way."

Once we'd arrived where the ceremony was to take place, I forcibly relaxed my fingers from the "oh-my-gosh-we're-gonna-die" handles attached to the frame of the car and flew to where my intended was pacing out front. I blew him a kiss as I hurdled the "Caution: Wet Floor" sign and yelled over my shoulder, "Gotta go—I'm running late!"

With the help of four bustling and *very* busy little old ladies, I was ready in thirty-eight seconds. Starting towards the door, I tripped on my hemline's lace and lunged for the arm of Phyllis, the most militant, geriatric gnome of the four. She grabbed my hand and with horror stared at my unpolished nails. She adjusted her dentures and then . . .

She whistled and called, "Now Mayva, and Merna,
and Effie, COME HERE!

Get the 'Purity in Pink' and a top coat—make it
clear!"

Two each dashed to a hand and whipped out the
bottles.

Great haste was made and not one lady dawdled.

Mayva and Merna polished away, while Effie fixed
cuticles and blew.

Head lady Phyllis looked on with satisfaction, for they
all knew what to do.

When the last nail was done and ruffles in place,

They placed the veil on my head and tugged it down
over my face.

With a shove to my backside and push towards the
door,

There were no more hands bustling. They had com-
pleted their chore.

With grace under fire, Phyllis called out my name,

"Now, Stacy, don't disappoint!" I flatly stared at the
dame.

With moments to go till my appointment at the altar,

I looked around, panicked, and then it was my turn to
falter—

"I have to go the bathroom," I said with a sigh.

Shielding her lips to Merna she said, "She's *lucky* to
have this guy!"

Then with absolute resolve, thrust me out the door,
not caring one little bit.

And as she closed it, whispered quite emphatically,
"Deary, *hold it!*"

We made it through the ceremony. Everyone was a bit stunned
when Brad, got a bad case of the hiccups half way through, but
on the whole, it was a beautiful service. Afterwards we had the

opportunity to mingle a bit, be kissed, squeezed, and given every bit of obscure advice on marriage that is known to man (and woman) all the way from Maine to Zimbabwe.

Ironically, I only faintly remember Brad's mom chastising Brad for kicking my train around the room instead of picking it up.

"But, Mom, it's in the way!" he hissed through gritted teeth.

"I know, dear, but her train is kind of like the family dog. It's a pain in the neck and always in the way, but you love it anyway and treat it with respect."

I should have listened a little closer and cherished that moment a bit more because that tidbit of advice—minus the dog—is what has pretty much summed up our entire marriage.

Life Lesson Number Eight:

※※※

The best things in life are worth all the pain and misery it takes to claim them as your own.

Baking Time Is Over

Our first son joined us almost two years after marriage and thus began the age of joy, embarrassment, boundless energy (his . . . *not* mine), sleepless nights, pride, neurosis, confusion, flashes of understanding, psychosis, spit up, Pepto-Bismol, and night-lights.

They did not necessarily come in that order though.

It all began with the conception of an illusion. I had envisioned myself sitting in a hospital bed smiling demurely (and yes, perfect hair, makeup, and freshly painted coral nails with an active-length, square-cut acrylic finish were included in this fantasy) with this adorable child nestled in my arms. Everyone around was cooing and professing that a more perfect and sweet baby had never been born. The Holy Mother herself would have been jealous of my sweet bundle of perfection who, by the way, was only a few moments old.

Obviously, I had missed the chapter on human reproduction in my home economics class. Mom tried describing the childbearing process to me. This cram session went something like this:

MY QUESTION: "Is it like sweet and sour sauce or grapefruits and sugar? You know that kinda good, kinda bad taste you get in your mouth but more specifically in terms of physical discomfort?"

HER ANSWER: "I'm not sure if I could classify it that way. Tell you what, try this approach. I'll show you how it feels to bear down in transition. Pull your lower lip out as far as you can and hold it there for a minute. Now stretch it out a little further . . . How does that feel?"

MY COMMENT: "Wow, that's it? That's not bad. I can handle this.

HER COMEBACK: "Wait a minute. I didn't say you were done. Now rip that lip up over your head and pull it down to kiss your backside. That's more what it's like."

Being the oldest of six children, I didn't pay much attention to such things as pain, afterbirth, and spinal blocks. I simply enjoyed the fruits of mom's labors as she brought home my favorite forms of entertainment. Babies were every bit as cool as puppies—cute and cuddly when they're little and *soooo* much fun to tease as they get older. My brothers even played fetch and tug of war after I'd confiscated something they wanted. I wasn't a constant tormentor, however. I only put them through the paces of such games when I was extremely bored or there was nothing on TV.

Actual conception shattered my illusions rather abruptly though. One day, Brad came home from the office just in time to see me turn green, wave, and dash to the bathroom. I came out wiping some residual guacamole sauce from the corner of my mouth and muttered, "I think something got lost in the translation from our fantasy to my pathetic reality."

He plucked a renegade French fry from the crease between my eyebrows. "I'm just glad it's you and not me." And with that, he sauntered off to fix himself a hamburger.

For the next eight months, I existed somewhere between misery over the swollen ankles and feet which looked like overgrown sea lions and euphoria over the fifty-two pound mass my ob-gyn called a healthy seven to eight pound fetus.

The irony of me not seeing or feeling my feet and this parasite being called a fetus did not escape me. In an age of clever marketing where corporate geniuses stick an "r us" on the end of nouns hoping to attract specific groups, I think the medical community should have named unborn children something that made more sense like "bellies r us," "acid indigestion r us" or even "Shamu r us." I admit, I scoffed several times at the notion that they were named after an anatomical extremity you couldn't even see. It was ludicrous!

I started to see a pattern in calculations and delivery date delusions amongst friends and casual acquaintances, who were or had experienced the early flutterings of motherhood. All of them would count by weeks until approximately sixteen to twenty weeks, at which point they would start counting by months. I've always been lousy at math, but even I could figure this one out.

Every female knows that you start counting weeks on the first day after your last cycle so at any given time you are technically two weeks along, actual conception aside. This is one of those unspoken truths that is known amongst women, but no one ever actually verbalizes. I have wondered if the "silent code" remains intact because saying such things aloud erases romance from the moment, or if it is simply because that to do so, would force us to quit living in our delusions. I personally think it is the latter.

Back to calculating. One month equals approximately four weeks but if you were to go the whole time by this equation, nine months would turn into ten and that thought is unbearable. However, if you are two weeks along at any given time, then six weeks is really four and eight is really six and so forth and so on. So in order to cope, women will go by weeks until about sixteen weeks to make the pregnancy seem further along than it really is and then past that time, will switch to months so that it doesn't seem like you will be pregnant until the next new millennium.

It is all just a simple self-preservation equation, created by twisting and manipulating math facts because they don't lie. (Math facts, not women.) Thus pregnant women everywhere can go on living a deluded life believing that it really isn't that long until they can reclaim their bodies.

I was in my, what seemed to be 298th week of pregnancy (technically I was six months, three weeks, four days, 18 hours, 36 minutes and forty-two seconds along, but who's counting?) when I began to realize how I could benefit tremendously from medical science! Medicine had come so far that babies who were born the size of a beanie baby were now growing into healthy productive adults!

I began feeling the stirrings of a phenomenon known to mothers everywhere simply as "cutting the apron strings." Whether I could technically classify my feelings as prepartum or post was yet undetermined but I knew that if Baby Anderson was born soon, it'd survive. Conversely, I was seriously beginning to wonder if I had a chance at survival if I had to go through another two months of bloated misery! I wondered that every day for the next two and a half months.

A week before my due date, I became a spigot of amniotic fluid which leaked every time I laid down and then got back up. I didn't know whether to call my doctor or Roto-Rooter. I finally called my doctor who told me I had a small hole in my amniotic sac and that I would in all likelihood go into labor at any moment. I was elated! I went to bed every night with my makeup touched up and my hair done, lying awake chanting "now is the time, now is the time".

Baby Anderson never got the hint.

Ten days later, I was admitted into the hospital for induction. My water never broke, I never dilated and Baby A got distressed being stuck in the birth canal. Mom got hysterical. Doc slipped Mom an I.V. mickey, and she went out for the count as they performed a c-section.

The next day the nurse brought me this wailing bundle, which looked like an oversized fly larvae with a red face. I gave it back.

"This isn't mine."

"Sure it is, Mrs. Anderson, it's your son." A son? She almost had me there as my curiosity pushed me to take a peek. I shoved him back. He was still wailing and his face was scrunched. He had grandpa sideburns and a conical head that would do any street cone proud. I was destined for a perfect child, and this certainly wasn't it!

"I want cold hard proof." Just then my husband walked in and announced with the pride of a man who had just cloned himself and with the humility and demureness of a WWF World Title wrestler, "There's my son!"

I slouched in my sheets, feeling completely inadequate and overwhelmed and mumbled, "I should've gotten a dog." The nurse looked at me waggling her disapproving eyebrow and then handed the wailing larvae to my giddy counterpart as she let her comments drift towards me. "He must take after your wife with his sweet disposition and all."

I didn't see the nurse again until she came to check the incision across my pelvic region. I was rather curious to see it myself, not having yet seen the "ole bod" yet without baby. I handed my son to Brad (I was actually coming to like the little guy and beginning to feel repentant for the dog comment) and lifted up my gown.

I screamed.

The nurse stumbled back caught quite off guard by my shrieking. "What is wrong with my skin?"

The nurse smiled and patted my arm, saying not a word while I hyperventilated. She then quickly went about her duties as I stared with horror at my tummy. Apparently genetics and pregnancy had had the last laugh.

They'd left me with an eight-pound four-ounce baby boy and a midsection that looked like a shar-pei.

Life Lesson Number Nine:

Never say or do anything that you would not want repeated in large groups of people you already have an inferiority complex toward.

Welcome to Motherhood U

I tiptoed into the corner of our apartment which served as nursery/office/guest bedroom/study and storage room, looked into the white and pink floral accented crib and stared at him with amazement. I could not believe that this sweet little guy, whom we'd named Justin, had survived the first three months with me! Just to make sure that my perfect record had not been broken, I stuck a hair up his nose. A small fist flew up to ferociously rub at it until there was no feeling left whatsoever. Good, he was still alive.

I was so proud of him! I wanted to show him to the world! I did the next best thing. I entered him into the State Fair livestock competition!

Just kidding. His father on numerous occasions, however, proudly declared to anyone who was listening that our son could've easily competed in the young stud classification. He would then hold up a size four diaper and nod with a knowing wink to every male within an eighth of a mile. I didn't have the heart to tell him that his son wore big diapers because his bladder took after my side of the family and could produce enough moisture to cure the Sahara's drought.

Instead, we took him to dinner. We were supposed to go to a movie afterwards, but Junior had other plans.

We had barely given our order when I heard a low, gurgling, bluup-like sound. My husband looked at me with aghast and said flatly, "You could've excused yourself to the bathroom. I wouldn't have minded."

"That wasn't me. I thought it was you."

"Not even. What was it then?"

"It sounded like Grandma's simmering chili before it erupts."

"Do you think . . . ?" We both looked at our son as his little face turned a deeper shade of purple with the exertion of his job. "Holy cow!" my husband exclaimed. "Did you know such sounds could come from that little of a guy?"

"I do now." I picked the baby up only to see that he had green slime dripping from his backside. I whispered emphatically for Brad to hand me the diaper bag and a blanket so I could try and conceal the mess. Brad just sat there dumbfounded while the mess continued to bubble out the gaps of his diaper and onto my white pants.

"What in tarnation? Where is it all coming from? What is wrong with him?"

"Think of him as an overachiever!" I hissed caustically. "Now hand me the blanket and diaper bag!" By this time it had run down my leg and seeped into my sandal. I wrapped our tot up with the expertise of a butcher wrapping a rump roast and sprinted for the car.

A box of 150 wipes, three outfits and an hour and 15 minutes later, Brad showed up to see me passed out in the back of our hatch back with the baby asleep in the crook of my arm. I barely lifted my head. "This would be a lot easier if he would do his duty every day instead of once a quarter. And to think I actually *thought* we'd been gifted with a perfect son who wasn't full of—"

"Cynical. You are so cynical. Remember he's just an overachiever." He wiped some crusty pea-green remnant off my cheek with a corner of the least-used wet wipe and sat down on the bumper next to me. "I figured you weren't coming back, so I had the waitress wrap up your dinner." He handed me a half eaten burrito with a few shreds of wilted lettuce on the side.

"Where's the rest of it."

"I gave it to the guy whose wife booked it on out of there after their eighteen-month-old gagged herself with a churro and spewed macaroni all over their dinner plates. Shame, it was still hot. I could see the steam from the next table over . . . their dinner—not the macaroni," he clarified when I looked at him with mild disgust.

"I met her. She's the one passed out in the red Accord over there."

Unfortunately that day was not the highlight of my most embarrassing moments in my young son's life. That distinction had to go to the day when Justin dressed up in his little sailor suit and went door-to-door selling rocks. I had naively thought he was pretending to be the captain of his Lil' Tykes ship sandbox but, nooo, he'd been out making a living.

He rushed in the door, beaming ear to ear and exposing four holes where teeth had been (he'd wiggled them until they fell out from sheer exhaustion—the teeth, not my son). Justin spilled the contents of his miniature briefcase out onto the family room floor. I looked at him with awe. The kid had obviously hit the jackpot out in that sand box. I ran to get my sneakers.

"Momma, where you goin'?"

"To get shoes and a metal detector. We're going back to the sand box."

"But, Mom, I didn't get this from the sand box." Uh-oh, that was not what I wanted to hear.

"Then, sweetheart, where did you get all this money?"

"I sold the rocks I dug out of the garden."

"Sweetie, people don't pay little boys this much money for plain old rocks."

"They did when I told them that I wanted to go to Disneyland like my mommy and daddy had promised but were too poor to keep their promise." With that, he lowered his eyes, slumped his shoulders, and threw out his lower lip while making a sad, frowny face.

His lip, at that moment, rivaled Reginald's.

"I see. Do you have any more rocks that I could buy?"

"No, but I could go dig up another one. Do you need a small one or a big one?"

"Big. I need it to use as a headstone for your grave when your father and I get done with you." At least I then knew why he was pulling his teeth for financial gain.

I must admit that my child was resourceful, especially when he knew exactly what he wanted. I came down the stairs one day just in time to see him swan dive off the banister, onto the couch, bounce onto my mini-tramp and soar through the air to the hutch, where he stuck like he was covered in Velcro. He then scrambled up two shelves to the candy jar that held the butter mints he loved so much, grabbed a fistful, and then slid down the TV antennae until he could safely drop to the floor.

He was a little over two at the time.

Before I was able to ship him off to public school for an education, he had tutored me in several areas of educational and character excellence. Matter of fact, he taught me one of the most important lessons I have ever learned when it comes to dealing with children: never, and I mean NEVER, let them hear anything you wouldn't want them to repeat in front of clergy or the in-laws.

I had worked for months trying to get him to take out his binky and learn how to talk.

"Common, Sweetie, just say momma or dada or even baba. I'm getting tired of trying to figure out what you want when you point in a general direction. I have lumps and bruises from the flying objects you've hurled back at me when I guessed wrong. *Please, just say something!* ANYTHING! I will even talk slower and e-nun-ci-ate for you."

I felt like Jim Carey as I slowly and laboriously mouthed out each syllable and sound with exactness for his visual and hopefully audible stimulation. He just looked at me blankly, continuing to suck on his mouth cork. In a moment of frustration, I got up off the floor, threw his teddy bear into the crib, and said in what I thought was an inaudible, if not completely indiscernible, "This is—" and a most colorful expletive.

The following Sunday in our women's study group, I had him sitting quietly on my lap sucking away on his pacifier when the teacher got up and announced the subject of the day's lesson: Profanity in the Home Drives the Spirit of Peace Away.

My darling child chose that exact moment to discard his pacifier with a propulsion force of negative two Gs into the back of old lady Whitmore's dual-colored basket weave beehive and animatedly fling his arms in circles while bouncing and repeating in a loud and amazingly clear voice, the expletive I had said.

I retrieved his pacifier (oh, how I wish it would've pacified him until at least church was over!) from between structural loops twelve and thirteen, and did the only thing that was left for me to do. I picked him up and marched him right on out while declaring in an equally loud and clear voice, *"I'm going to have a long serious talk to your father about his potty mouth!"*

Life Lesson Number Ten:

❦

Never let fear and outside influences inhibit you, thus keeping you from conquering your ambitions.

Would You Like Flood Insurance with That?

We were a real family now. As such, since it is a natural desire for humans to want to leap to the next plateau of progress, I naturally wanted to put down roots and capture the whole American dream. You know the one. It includes 2.3 kids (or if you live in Utah like I do, 5.9), the white picket fence surrounding a modest 5800 square-foot, two-story stucco with accent rock, and a family dog. I thought about a four-car garage and an impressive water feature, but I didn't want my humble abode to be too ostentatious.

I, however, missed one small detail in my oversimplified equation—you had to actually qualify for the thirty-year mortgage. Thus our search was narrowed down significantly to the three bedroom, two bath, 2200 square foot brick ramblers with two car garages.

After looking at our income, our agent virtually cut our list down to nothing. Our choices became the quaint little town home next to a crack house in the slums, which needed a few cosmetic improvements, or a 1300 square foot repossessed tri-level in the suburbs that had . . . uh, well . . . potential.

The latter had a fireplace (which was a great resale feature) and a rather fragrant lilac bush right under the master bedroom window.

I fell in love while Brad gave it a barely passing score. Since women can be rather persuasive when they want to be, I won the debate, and we signed the papers on Friday—after declining the additional flood insurance—and called it home.

It's a good thing that the fireplace was in working order because three days after moving in, the gas company condemned our furnace. We also found out that the phone lines had been cut, the sprinkling system had a leak, which resulted in our front yard looking like the banks of the Mississippi River during its worst flood season ever, and a nice little family of skunks had somehow infiltrated the crawl space and decided to also make it their home.

Apparently they had grown quite fond of their dank digs because when Brad tried to bribe them into the open with some tasty vittles, they let him have it. He stunk so bad, I made him sleep on the deck between the lawn mower and some broken pots on a lounge chair, procured during a K-Mart blue light special, for a week.

There were a couple of bright spots, however.

1. The color scheme could (and *would*) be easily changed.
2. There were wood floors under the carpet that was full of pet dander and leftover lint from the 1930s.
3. And between the kitchen faucet that blew off when the water was turned on and the steady leak in the roof that drizzled every time it rained or the swamp cooler was on, I did get a pretty elaborate water feature that consisted of a four-ft fountain and a waterfall!

We couldn't wait to show our parents! The looks on their faces said everything—as long as the roof didn't cave in, we had a project that would keep us out of their hair and basements for a good long time.

We were busy little bees. We tore out carpets, painted over the pistachio green, pink, and purple walls, took apart all of the plumbing, replaced the broken doorjambs and doorknobs, temporarily patched the roof, ripped out and glued down new linoleum in the kitchen, and sanded the floor down to the natural grain and resealed it.

Then Monday came and Brad decided he'd better go back to work, so he could get a break from his honey-do list and find a way to pay for all of my rather zealous plans. The only problem was that the plumbing still wasn't working.

He zipped over to his parents to shower. Hah! And to think they actually thought that home ownership and perpetual projects would keep us away.

Monday night when he got home, he found a cold Arby's sandwich on the table with a note that said, "I'm upstairs working and Justin is watching a video. Come on up when you get home. Love you, Stacy."

I'm not sure why I bothered with the note. I heard him mutter, "Great, I wonder what she's up to now," before taking two steps and leaping up the rest of the stairs in one bound (there were only five). He found me in the bathroom sporting a pair of steamed up goggles, a chisel in one hand and a hammer in the other and remnants of concrete and tile clinging to my bangs and ponytail. He looked at Justin who shrugged and then turned back to his movie.

"What in heaven's name are you doing?"

"Isn't it obvious?" And just to make sure he figured it out, I whacked the chisel into another piece of tile that catapulted off the wall and went flying in the direction of Brad's head. He ducked as it sailed past his left shoulder.

"Do you, by any chance, know how to retile that once you're done?"

"No, of course not. I just thought we'd figure it out together after you got home from work."

"Of course, you did," he said mockingly and went to change his clothes.

I can safely group all of my projects into two categories: the first being projects that I was able to complete before Brad got home for work also known as the "Day Projects or DPs," and those which I was able to complete once he got home, also known as the "Night Projects or NPs." I would have called them evening projects but they usually went *well* into the night. We were a great team.

Granted, he was usually the one who completed them, but I was the one who was able to cross them off my list. That had to account for something.

On Tuesday my DPs consisted of tearing up the lawn, finding and unburying all of the sprinkler pipes that were hiding, and making a horde of wasps angry as I tried to knock down their nest from the crevice between the shed and the carport wall. The NPs were leveling and reseeding the lawn (sod was too expensive), fixing, testing and pressurizing the sprinkling system, whose control box was by the crevice between the shed and the carport, while avoiding the wasps that had suddenly become quite territorial.

Brad lost a few battles, so I added a trip to the store for Benadryl and Calamine lotion to my NP list and accomplished that one all by myself.

On Wednesday, I tore all the cabinet doors off the hinges and sanded them down. Unfortunately I used a belt sander with coarse paper thinking I'd get the job done in half the time. It left some terrible grooves which took Brad all night to smooth out before he could revarnish and reinstall them.

Thursday, I stripped all the caulking, broke a window while trying to put up new blinds, papered the nook, and stenciled a sunflower vine in the bathroom, which turned out pretty good if I do say so myself.

Brad caulked, patched the window, put up the blinds, and got the air bubbles out of the paper. He dropped to his knees, clasped his hands, and thanked God mightily when he saw my sunflower vine didn't need help.

By Friday I was tired. Besides, I couldn't find much more to do other than the electrical, which Brad had already put me under legal contract and threat of financial boycott if I touched. I remedied the boredom by coming up with my next big project. When Brad came home, I smiled sweetly and put my arms around his neck.

"Please don't tell me you screwed up the electrical. Anything but the electrical! You *do* remember that we have an agreement, don't you?"

"It's not the electrical."

"Then what is it?"

"I added a job to your NP list." He rolled his eyes and with a groan turned to his closet to fetch his grubbies.

"Not so fast, Studmuffin." I pulled him back. "We need to work on another little project . . ." I saw a glint in his eye as he caught my drift. It disappeared rather quickly only to be replaced with a look of worry and stress.

"Does this mean that we'll have to remodel the basement too?"

Life Lesson Number Eleven:

Some of life's biggest joys are found in the most unexpected places. You just have to recognize the sunshine within.

Dandelions Have Feelings Too

Nine months and a remodeled basement later, our second son, arrived with a whoosh and a squirt. Other than the fact that I measured out at forty-two weeks when I was only thirty-four along (I begged my doctor to use months instead of weeks, but he laughed and said either way, I still had a darn long time to go), the pregnancy was, for the most part, pretty uneventful.

Three weeks before my due date, the doctor, convinced that I was having twins, booked me for an ultrasound and an amniocentesis. I was so weary of dragging my belly around that I didn't have enough sense to be scared or even slightly nervous. I should have been. I'd never seen a needle that long before!

I reached for Brad's hand and grasped . . . air? I looked over the side of the gurney only to see him passed out on the floor. Apparently the needle had bothered him also. Once my man, who heretofore had branded himself as my "extra source of strength through this ordeal," was out in the hall, comfortably holding his head between his knees and practicing breathing techniques, the doctor came back and pulled out the needle and an iodine pack. I sighed and averted my gaze from the needle to the doctor's name badge and tried to relax by concentrating on it using it as my focal point.

Oh, my laws! Does it really say what I think it says? It did. Reading it again didn't give me any comfort. It said "Dr. Jekyll."

I flew off the gurney, making a cross with my fingers and telling him to back off as I tried to pry open the door with my bare butt cheeks. Seriously! Who could trust a guy with a license given to him by a medical board, who apparently thought it okay to authorize people with seven-inch needles named Dr. Jekyll to practice in the state of Utah?

Dr. Jekyll motioned for his nurse to move in, cutting off my escape path while he called for reinforcements. I might have made a clean escape (albeit cheeks flapping in the wind) if an anesthesiologist's office had not been right next door. I think I went on record as being the first patient to have needed general anesthesia for an amniocentesis, at least in Dr. Jekyll's practice.

When I came to, I was given my instructions and told to call later for the results of my L/S ratio which, my doctor said, would indicate the baby's lung maturity. It came back a 3.2 which meant that his lungs were well done. He was so ripe, in fact, my doctor said that he'd come out wanting the car keys. (For the record, Justin— who at age four wanted me to legally change his middle name to Ford and has already put a clause in his will stating that he wants to be buried in a 1957 Peacock blue Ford Thunderbird—was the one who came out wanting the car keys).

There was a whoosh as my water broke in the middle of the grocery store, saturating my ankle socks. Within a few hours and many pain killers later, Mitchell entered the world and promptly squirted the doctor and three of the attending nurses. He has been known as my "whiz kid" ever since.

He had intelligence that put Einstein to shame. He had a finely tuned sense of justice that would've brought a tear to Strom Thurman's eye. He had a work ethic that would've made General Patton lower his head in humility. He had a sense of territory and expansion which would have toppled the Romans and an understanding of sovereign domain which would've made the ancient Egyptians whip themselves instead of their slaves. He had the will to persevere and matched it with his incredible persistence. Thomas Edison, who had failed miserably so many times before he finally succeeded, could've taken a lesson or two out of my son's book. He was happy, smiled *all* the time, and much to my dismay, had the vocabulary and quick wit to rub it in my face.

Although I felt constantly inferior and dimwitted compared to this child, I did find the things that were unique and lovable about him. He was my dandelion, the family weed, which just kept coming back again and again. I have to admit that at times however, had it not been for those moments of radiant sunshine that are perfectly symbolized by the bright, fuzzy flowers, which bring a decorum of joy to grassy pastures, I would've used Roundup on him.

Giving him full credit though, there were those times when he knew how to use his intelligence in such a way that it made one stand back in awe and wonder why he hadn't thought of it first. His first exposure to public speaking was just such an occasion.

He had barely turned three when he got the assignment in Sunday school to speak on the Bible story of Meshach, Shadrach, and Abed-nego, and the fiery furnace. Apparently, he'd been the only child who could pronounce their names correctly. I was so proud! This would be one area where he could shine. We worked all week on his talk, the timing for his visual aids, and put together graphs and comparison charts. He was ready to go.

Unfortunately, I was running late again.

I dropped him off before making a mad dash to the church library to acquire the main visual aid for my son's presentation. I made it back in time to hand him the picture and hear Sister Baxter who was conducting, announce the program. "And after that, Mitchell Anderson will then give us his talk."

The scripture and prayer were given and then she motioned for my son to step up to the miniature pulpit. He took his stance and with a dramatic air, looked around his juvenile audience as I waited with baited breath amongst the other proud parents in the back of the room. Maybe he had a future in politics . . .

He leaned slowly into the microphone staring straight ahead to the children in the middle row and with a reverent voice said, "I will now give my talk to you." And with that, he picked up all of his stuff, walked into the audience, and handed Jimmy his picture, Tony his graphs, Jenny his comparison chart, Byron his other picture, and Stephanie the verbiage for his presentation. He then moved on through the rest of the row and took a seat next to his teacher. He leaned in her direction and looking so proud of himself said, "I was glad Sister Baxter said I could give my talk to them. I didn't want to do the stupid thing anyway."

I stood in the back mortified until the guy next to me whistled and said, "I wish I would've thought of that before I gave my speech at the law school commencement exercises last week. I bet his was a lot easier to prepare and he managed to keep the audience awake."

As he got older, there were days when I just wanted to throttle him! He was Bill Gates in a prepubescent's body. When he desired something, he lived by the creed that if he was persistent and asked one more time before I tore my hair out and rent my clothes, he had an 85 percent chance of getting what he wanted.

"You know, Mitch, you are like a woodpecker sitting on my nose, pecking the tarnation outta my forehead and boring into my senses."

"Ha ha, that was cute. So, Mother, can I have Justin's vintage police car?"

"Go away, Mitch."

"But you said, Mom, that if we didn't put our toys away, anyone else could call dibs on them."

"It was in his room, Mitch, on his nightstand."

"It rolled off and one wheel was out the door. In my opinion, that classifies under the move it or lose it rule."

"You're playing with incidentals. You're too harsh. You need to relax a bit and learn when to give an inch."

"And you're the one who told me last week when I took all of the money out of your wallet to buy ice cream for the kids in the neighborhood that there are no shades of gray when it comes to theft and certain rules. It's either black or white. You were very adamant about that."

I dismissed him with a wave of my hand and figured I could drive back to Phoenix for another car easier than I could win this fight.

Later I went into his room to look at him while he was sleeping, just so I could ponder an illusion of a child that gave me peace. He was grinning in his sleep. I couldn't believe it. He was mocking me from behind those closed eyelids! I would try again tomorrow.

I decided to take him along while I walked the dog through the park so I could chat with him. There was something I needed to discuss with him anyway.

"Sweetheart, do you like Grandma being one of the teachers at your school?" He nodded yes. "Good, she likes being there too, but she's a little concerned that some of the other teachers might think she is older than dirt if they keep overhearing you call her 'Grandma.' Could you maybe think of something else to call her at school?" He nodded yes again, and just as I was congratulating myself for having won this round rather painlessly, the sprinklers went on.

I must digress here in order to tell you that our springer spaniel fancied herself an aquatic being. I'm pretty sure with about 98 percent certainty that when she lounged in the sun out back on our deck moaning in her sleep, she was actually day dreaming about being the Little Mermaid. How she loved the water! She took off in a blur dragging me behind, with my wrist tangled in the leash trying to keep up with her enthusiastic water ballet.

After the eight ten-minute cycles were over, I returned to my son, who was literally rolling on the ground, laughing and pointing his finger at me. "What do you two think you are, amphibians or something?" We walked back home while the sound of sneakers slurping upon the pavement reverberated through the night sky.

The next morning, I asked him if he remembered what we had talked about the night before. He nodded and headed off to school. As he headed down the fourth-grade hall on his way to the kindergarten room, he ran into my mother and all the other teachers coming out of a staff meeting.

Motherhood is, for the most part, a pretty thankless job. That is why one generation will wish the arguments, sleepless nights, and embarrassing moments upon the next. You see, misery DOES love company in this instance. However, there are those few precious times in life where this curse backfires and makes it all worthwhile. This was one of those moments.

With delight and a voice that echoed down every hall in the school he yelled, "Hey there, Woman! Just between you and me, you don't look older than dirt! Maybe fire, but not dirt."

I guess I did get my mom back for the Reginald stunt after all.

Life Lesson Number Twelve:

Diversity is what makes the whole of humanity sparkle and shine ever so brilliantly.

How to Tour the Pacific without Crossing an Ocean

I knew I was in trouble from the day my third son, Josh, was born. Something about my whole hospital experience with him screamed doom and chaos. I think it pretty much spiraled out of control somewhere between the mild earthquake and the island of Samoa moving into my room. Allow me to elaborate.

After my third C-section, I snuggled into my bed with the delicious sleepiness that comes from finally taking a well-deserved sabbatical from pregnancy. No more bathroom breaks every twenty minutes through the night. A cessation to aches in my back. And a night of blissful sound sleep with the aid of the modern day miracle we call pain medication. I was going to enjoy my stay in this brand new hospital. I had toured it the week before during an open house and had thought what a fine facility it was! Surely good enough to bear my son in.

I was abruptly and ever so rudely interrupted from my encroaching slumber by a nurse dumping a quart of ice water onto my lap. She'd knocked it off of my rolling table with her ample backside as she pulled a gurney with an even more ample Polynesian woman into the space labeled Bed A.

"Cheerio!" she sing-songed in an annoyingly bright tone for two in the morning. "You have a roommate, Mrs. Anderson. We'll get that nasty little spill wiped up in a minute."

The staples in my incision had rusted before they brought back a dry gown and sheets.

I looked over at my new roommate in Bed A and happily noted that she was sound asleep. This won't be too bad I thought and closed my eyes once again. I woke 10 minutes later to my IV pole animatedly trotting down the tile floor. That's rather odd I mused as I reeled it back in by the drip line.

There was a crackle over the loud speaker as an announcement about a code blue sliced through the night. I couldn't hear the message in its entirety though because the young nurse in the hall was running back and forth in a panic yelling, "How am I going to get all these people out of here! Half of them can't even walk!"

With that, an older lady, whom I supposed was her supervisor, put an arm around her shoulder, whispered something into her ear and then casually walked off. The young nurse looked at her wide eyed and bolted in the opposite direction. I suddenly did not feel comforted by my surroundings anymore.

The announcement once again blared over the loud speaker, "Code Blue. Level Two. The elevators are shut off. Code Blue. Level Two. The elevators are shut off." I didn't even have time to think about the effects of those words on my increasingly fragile trust in this institution when I saw an orderly whiz by with a cart resembling an oversized car battery and jumper cable set. I could hear the cart crashing (no pun intended) KA-CHUNK, KA-CHUNK all the way down the stairs. Trying to keep myself calm by looking at the bright side of things, I thought about how life is full of ironies, and I quietly admitted that it is, at times, even better than fiction.

This whole farce had turned into a rather intriguing soap opera. I scooted up in bed for a better vantage point and waited with anticipation to see if the cart had made it in time or not. "Code Blue off. Return the cart. Elevators are now turned on. Code Blue off. Return the cart. Elevators are now turned on." I sunk back into my sheets wishing I could turn the night off. I needed a moment to mourn.

I was pondering the meaning of life and why on Earth a hospital would turn the elevators off when someone was struggling between life and death when the most bright intense white light I had ever seen shone through my window. It illuminated the whole room and made it radiate with what I thought to be a most holy incandescent glow.

"Wow!" I thought. "Mr. or Mrs. Code Blue sure is lucky to have such a send off!" I wondered why God in his infinite wisdom and compassion was allowing me to witness this special moment. Maybe it was to give me comfort that all was and would be well.

I raised the head of my bed to its highest point so I could peer out the window. My stomach muscles had been severed so sitting up on my own, let alone walking, wasn't yet an option. There, sitting in front of me, was the life flight helicopter in all of its mechanical and sobering glory. I stared at the pilot. He smiled, waved, and gave me a thumbs up. I lowered my bed. So much for being comforted.

I nestled back into my pillow just as Bed A's husband came through the door and, noticing that his wife was asleep, decided to give me their family history. I could've been a bit more charitable if he'd *only* tutored me in the chronological timeline of the island he'd been born on, but he went through every inbreeding case on every Pacific island and who begat whom from the days of Adam and Eve to the present.

Finally as the sun was breaking over the horizon, I decided that I needed medication and sanity rapidly! The pain in my gut was growing larger than his family tree and I was losing my happy demeanor quicker than Elvis's hips in the early days. I was pounding ferociously on the nurse's call button when the nurse showed up and gave sleeping Bed A a pain shot and left. I pounded once again. The nurse returned, looked at Bed A still sleeping, and noted to her husband that she was a rather large woman, so a second dose, she supposed, would be okay. She gave her another shot. He never said a word but just nodded. Why did he have to shut up now? I kicked the call button with my foot. The nurse once again appeared and told Bed A's husband that she couldn't have another shot. Two was the maximum dose, even for as large a woman as she.

Dragging myself almost out of bed, I ripped open the curtain and yelled, "ME, YOU DIMWIT! IT'S ME! I WANT MY DRUGS NOW!"

The nurse quickly stepped to the side of my bed closing the curtain again and in a hushed tone said, "Well, Mrs. Anderson, no sense in being cranky. All you needed to do was press your call button. I would've happily given you your meds. Now is there anything else that you need?"

"Yes, a muzzle for that man and an answer to a question."

"That's quite rude! He seems rather quiet to me. What's your question?"

"How come you turn off the elevators during a code blue?"

"We don't."

"You did last night. I heard it over the PA system"

"There was a 5.1 earthquake last night. We turn off the elevators during earthquakes or fires. I'm surprised you were that sleepy during the tremors. There was quite a hullabaloo around here from what the swing shift nurses said. They must've needed a crash cart to wake you this morning if you sleep that soundly." She turned and jauntily strode out the door.

"I wouldn't have counted on it getting here on time," I mumbled.

By the time the meds were supposed to kick in, they couldn't. My nerves were wound tighter than strings on a Louisiana banjo and they were about to be plucked rather harshly.

If hearing that Mr. Bed A's family accounted for three fourths of the South Pacific's populous didn't make me a believer, then seeing was truly believing. They all moved in to our hospital room that day. Their children were crawling under my bed. Their cousins were putting their overnight bags in my closet. Their uncles were sitting on my bed while their aunts were giving me tips on how to breast feed. It was less of a miracle when Moses parted the Red

Sea than it was for Brad to part the ocean of Polynesia to get to my bedside. There were streams and hordes of them. I prayed for night to come and for my next shot of Demerol. I seriously considered asking the nurse if she could upgrade the dose to the size of a Big Gulp.

When night finally did come, Bed A's hubby decided to stay and sleep in a lounge chair that he'd placed between our beds so his wife had easier access to the bathroom. I don't think it even crossed his mind that I'd had to beat my bladder into submission all day so I wouldn't have to carve through the mass they called their family.

Oh well. I could handle just about anything as long as all was quiet so I could finally get some sleep. Quiet, or rather lack of, became a problem.

A sonic jet was quieter than this man! I'd never heard man or beast snore as loud as he! Why, he even surpassed the sound of the TV she had going at 39 decibels to drown out the wails of her newborn. I put a pillow on my head and tried to roll over. No use. My innards felt like they were going to tumble on out. I rolled back and tried to meditate blocking out the pandemonium. That's when his thick hairy arm came through the curtain and landed across my chest.

Pain or not, I ran around the corner and down the hall to the payphone and called Brad collect.

"Mmmm . . . hello." How dare he sound like I'd woken him up from a sound sleep!

"Come get me now or I'm goin' AWOL and walking home."

"Has your doctor released you?"

"He will or I'll sue." I hobbled back to my room after stopping in the public restroom. Never had an ice cold toilet seat felt so good.

I tiptoed past Bed A when I noticed with relief that her baby was asleep. I practically leapt into bed only to find an older woman who I assumed to be another twig on their family tree in my place. I screamed. The old woman barely opened her eyes before rolling over and going back to sleep. The baby started to wail again.

Bed A was generous enough to offer me a folding chair they'd confiscated from the waiting room area. "Sorry, we thought you were gone. My mother-in-law hasn't had much sleep." I could definitely relate.

She then introduced me to her baby who had weighed in at 12 lbs 14 oz. He was the most interesting small specimen of humanity I think I've ever seen. Typically, from what I've seen anyway, primates have more hair and larger brow lines than males from the human species but this infant certainly broke that rule easily enough. He had an unusually bountiful outcropping of silken strands which exploded from the top of his head and a ridge above his eye sockets that protected his visual acuteness better than any hockey mask ever would.

I looked at his nose and smiled. He was going to be a great athlete someday. I just knew it. His nostrils were perfectly made for inhaling mass quantities of oxygen for those moments of muscle hunger and quick exertion. I would've touched his cheek out of courtesy but was a little nervous that my hand would be sucked into one of those caverns called a nostril as he inhaled.

"You have the makings of a great football player there."

"Her name is Eunice Mawanda."

I gulped and cheesily grinned. I personally thought her baby girl with the inch-wide unibrow looked more like an Ima . . . as in Ima gonna be the first woman to make it as a linebacker in the NFL and give Refrigerator Perry a run for his money!

Life Lesson Number Thirteen:

Despite wishing otherwise, you are bound to deal with at least a few rather anal people over the course of your lifetime. In these cases, it's best to go with the flow and lend a helping hand.

Red Pants or Bust

Someone once told me that the difference between neurotics and psychotics is that neurotics build dream castles in the sky and psychotics are the ones who move in. I think it was the same guy who penned the phrase "Live in glass houses and throw rocks." Whoever he was, I am pretty sure he had a close and personal relationship with Josh.

Things were okay through the first year, and he was an angelic and delightful baby. Then, the day after he turned one, he reinvented himself. We renamed him Lucifer—you know, after the one brother who didn't get his way, so he threw a royal stink and has raised holy hell ever since. Yep, that pretty much sums up my Josh.

On our twenty-ninth visit to the Instant Care Center within his first 18 months of life, we had to fill out paperwork listing the new insurance we'd just enrolled with before our son could be treated. When the nurse asked who Josh's new primary care physician was, we stated that he, as of yet, did not have one under this new plan. Mitch was outraged at the complete and utter untruth of our response. "He does too have a doctor! We visit him quite frequently when Josh gets hurt. His name is Emergency Room."

All of those trips to the emergency room, however, did teach Josh a bit about medicine and diagnostics. When he was about five, he experienced a bad bout of intestinal flu which apparently scared and confused him. I had to explain to him about "yucky poo" being nature's way of flushing the bad stuff from our bodies. He looked at me and dashed to the bathroom yet again. After what seemed like an eternity, I knocked on the door.

"Josh, honey, are you okay?" The door slowly opened, and he stood there with a grin.

"I figured it out."

"Figured what out, Joshie?"

"What makes the 'yucky poo.' " I had to hear this one.

"What?" With that he dropped his drawers, twirled around, bent over, split his cheeks, pointed, and asked, "You see that big red dot? When you have the big red dot, you have 'yucky poo.' " Who was I to denounce his theories on cause and effect? Besides, in a round-about-moon-sort-of-way, he was right. He just had the cause and effect bit reversed I thought. He raced to the toilet yet again. I reached for the Balmex and Pepto-Bismol.

I peeped through the door crack and wedged my arm through, tossing the items to him. "Plaster this on that dot, and take some pink medicine. It'll go away in no time."

Josh was a child of extremes. His world was all or nothing. So when we got through the touchy-feely phase of his bowel movements, we headed into the can't-touch-this phase. Three times a day whether we wanted to or not, we would get "The Call." "Moooom, Daaad, come wipe my buuummm!" If at home, Brad and I would do rock-paper-scissors to determine who'd have to leave the dinner table to assist him in taking care of business. If we were out, it was Brad's duty. I couldn't go into a men's restroom, and no son of mine was going into a women's facility! A couple of times Brad tried to pay some stranger off, but the offer was usually refused.

From five on, every year before his birthday we'd talk to our son and tell him that it was time to grow up and handle his own business. He'd give us "the look" and say with feigned innocence,

"But I trust the way you do it. It makes me feel like I have nothing to hide."

"Son, when your pants are down around your ankles and you're mooning the world, you absolutely have nothing to hide."

"Just until my seventh birthday. That's only two weeks away!"

"Okay, but then not a day past!"

After we'd taken his birthday guests home, we took the family along with grandma and grandpa to Arby's. Half way through the meal, Josh got wide eyed and broke out into a sweat. His regularity was kicking in and he needed to clear a little space for what was coming in the top side. I winked at him and nodded in encouragement. "Go on, Josh, you can do it."

His dad showed his confidence in him by gesturing his head in the direction of the bathroom and winking. Josh squared his shoulders, lifted his chin, thrust out his chest, and walked down the long hall to face his destiny as an independent man. We listened as the words from a classic little ditty echoed down the hall into the dining area.

"When you're sittin' on the john, and the toilet paper's gone . . . Be a man! Use your hand and beeeeeee proouud."

Brad grinned. "That's my boy," he thumped his chest in mock pride.

"Oh good. He can share your fries then since he'll probably forget to wash his hands," I said and then smirked as my husband choked on his drink.

We waited anxiously. Brad paced the lobby (he was too antsy to sit still) while I did what came natural. I borrowed a dish rag from the girl behind the counter and wiped down every table, chair, bench, window, and blind in sight. I contemplated taking the drink machine apart but thought better of it. The syrup build-up would probably make me pass out. Ten minutes. Twenty. I leaned over to Brad and whispered, "Do you think he fell in? Maybe you should go check."

"Don't give up on him. He needs our trust and support now more than ever." Thirty minutes. Forty.

"Do you think waiting for the birth announcement of our first grandchild will be this nerve racking?"

"What do you mean? This is exactly like waiting for a birth announcement!" Just then, we heard the door creak open. We held our breath in anticipation. This was the moment we'd been waiting for . . .

"Daaad, come wipe my buuummmm!" Amid snickers and giggles from the dining patrons, Brad sauntered sheepishly to the bathroom. I rolled my eyes towards the ceiling. "Lord, please don't ever let him get into any big addictions," I prayed. "Rehabilitating him and getting him to do it independently would kill us."

The irony of my son was that other people's opinions mattered so much to him. Take, for example, the day I tried to get him to wear red pants to kindergarten. In an effort to avoid another episode of the modern and the mad, I put on my hat as the kindergarten Fashion Fairy and hung his clothes on his door before he woke up. I then stealthily backed out of the doorway before he could start hollering his disapproval. I liked playing Tooth Fairy better. At least I had a chance of winning when we haggled over the interest rates for a baby tooth.

Ten minutes before the school bell was supposed to ring, he was still standing in front of the ensemble I'd put together with a scowl on his face.

"What's wrong now, Josh?"

"No one wears red pants to school. They all wear jeans. Everyone in the whole flippin' class will laugh at me."

"No one will laugh. Besides you need to learn how to be a leader. Now put the pants on or you'll be late for school." He reluctantly did as I asked and then headed downstairs to eat his cereal. That had been too easy, WAY too easy I thought with distrust and a pit in my stomach. Seconds later, he came upstairs with a sizable wet circle in the general area of his groin. "What on earth did you do?"

"I had an accident. I guess I can't very well wear these to school now, can I?" He ran to get his favorite pair of jeans.

What do you say to a kid with no sense of reasoning? One who won't go to sleep in his room because he honestly believes in boogie men, who can break through wrought iron gates, scale two-story wood paneled houses, slither through double-pane windows that are open a quarter of an inch, shimmy through one inch blinds, and steal a kid away without waking anyone. Mind you, this is the same kid who will wander away in large malls. When asked what he'd do if a bad guy nabbed him, he strongly declared, "Kick him and beat him up, of course!" And he sincerely believes he can!

How do you apologize to his teacher because your son believes that he's incapable of doing his report on Russia because he's never been there and actually seen the Kremlin? Yet his favorite sport, the one he lives for and excels at, is played on frozen ponds in Canada while he worships and wants to grow up to be like the gods of hockey that hail from—you guessed it—Russia.

How does one deal with a child, who before his second birthday, has painted the basement walls, the washer, dryer and every white appliance with candy apple red nail polish; ironed a hole in the brand new carpet in the basement; gotten stuck up in a forty-foot tree that only the fire department can rescue him from; broken two dozen eggs on the kitchen floor practicing soft hockey hands and turned it into a slip-n-slide; and reduced his mother to tears every day for nine months straight?

You resist the urge to strangle him with whatever cord or article of clothing that is readily available at least one thousand, three hundred and forty seven times a day. That's how. It takes willpower, but it can be done.

I happened to be on the phone with my mother-in-law when I heard a faint choking/squeaking/gasping noise coming from an upstairs bedroom. With my cordless in tow, I leapt the stairs in a single bound and flew into his room where he had managed to twirl and waltz right off the side of his top bunk bed while his blind cord was wrapped around his neck. He was blue, hanging there lifeless. In one felling swoop, I ripped the blinds down with one hand and clutched him in the other. I instinctively recalled from the recesses of my memory the how-to manual on CPR. Breathing on his own again, he opened his eyes, coughed a few times, and mumbled, "I don't feel so good."

He then rolled over, slipping into peaceful slumber while I slid down the wall into a fetal position clutching the phone.

I needed solace from someone who could really understand my weariness and my overwrought nerves. Brad answered his work line after the receptionist had paged him.

"Hey, hon. What's going on?" I wasn't quite sure, but I thought I heard commotion and whispering in the background.

"What is all of that noise? It sounds like someone is breathing over your shoulder."

"Oh, no one. Just a bunch of people standing around. So, what's wrong? You sound weary. Is it Josh again?"

"Am I on speaker phone?"

"Back to the subject. What's happened?"

"Yes, it's Josh. Who else would make me this old so quickly? Are you sure I'm not on speaker phone? You sound hollow."

"Stace, continue."

"He finally did it. He went over the edge, literally." I recounted every horrible second, his little blue face, his lifeless body, my life-saving efforts, and the broken blind.

"Did you have to use CPR?"

"Yes, what does that—" That's when I heard the thunderous whoop, whistle, and applause in the background.

"Braaaad . . . what is going on?"

"Sorry, hon. Oscar just won the office pool. He bet Josh by strangulation, with a kicker if CPR was used"

That was when I learned that my son's antics and my fragile state of mind were providing fun, diversions, and a tax-free income to the people at my husband's work.

And he said he had the harder job!

Life Lesson Number Fourteen:

There is no substitute for a parent's teaching. Even Katie Couric, whose job is to inform, can't teach your children the values intrinsic to a happy childhood.

Is It Mid-morning Crisis or Am I Going Postal?

No one can tell me kids aren't observant and that the world of technology hasn't increased their awareness of the events taking place in the world around them. It happens at such an early age too! One day, they are sweet, little beings that have trust, bright smiles, and innocence, and within forty-eight hours after Santa has brought them an Xbox, they've turned into war mongers who rule the world with a joystick and a rumble pack.

Children can now virtually step into the boots of characters, ruling with iron fists and a bazooka on the screen, while the crustless peanut butter and jelly sandwich—that Mom had to make because they aren't allowed to use sharp objects yet—sits on a plate on the carpet next to them. The whole scene kinda makes you wonder just a bit.

I wanted my children to appreciate the world they lived in and view our neighborhood as a wonderful place to explore and grow up in rather than a killing field of the American ideals, which I hold so dear. This being the case, I decided that I needed to model those values and teach them some community spirit, so I popped some popcorn and invited them to sit down and take an interest in their world with me. In the three minutes I'd had the news on, the media journalist recounted the day's 84 violent crimes and 103 bombings across the globe. I promptly turned it off and decided to play Xbox with them. It was far less violent.

The next day Mitchell came home from school, dropped his backpack, got a glass of water, and then headed back out the door. I opened it back up and called to him, "Where are you going?"

"With Mr. Johnson. He's gunna let me help him deliver the mail." This was wonderful! At least one of my sons was learning that there was a profession out there where you could give freely, helping make the world a non-threatening, non-violent, overall better place to live.

For the next two years, Mitch would make the rounds with the postman after school and then do another route of his own later that evening. He'd deliver little notes and flyers he'd created, sorted and stamped on my 25 percent cotton stationary and linen business envelopes. He went through my entire year's stock of business supplies in the first week. Forced budgetary cuts signed into law by Mom forced him to start utilizing the cheaper one thousand envelopes for five dollars, scratch paper, and homemade stamps from then on.

When the postman retired, he gave Mitch one of his old uniforms. Mitch then confiscated one of my canvas shoulder bags so he could carry on as the youngest mail carrier to ever have donned the blue uniform. I helped him alter his new digs so they'd at least stay up concealing his vintage post stamp boxer shorts. I needn't have bothered. He proudly showed them to anyone who answered their door.

Mind you, he didn't actually work for the postal service. He was more like a mascot of sorts, spreading cheer and scraps of paper throughout the neighborhood while carrying on the fine tradition of delivering flyers I'd already thrown away and any samples I wasn't quick enough to hide before he got home from school.

One such day as he was sneaking a Bic razor enclosed in a sunny yellow box and a sample of shampoo and conditioner into his satchel, I caught his arm and reached into the bag retrieving my free toiletries. I also pulled out a fluorescent green water gun filled and ready to shoot.

"What is *this*? You'd better explain and explain *quick*, Mister, or I'm calling your father."

"Geez, Mom. I don't know what you're so bent over. It's the new craze. All the long standing mail carriers are carrying mail, samples, ads, and guns these days. I just wanted to be hip so I thought I'd go authentic postal today."

I grabbed his wrist and dragged him upstairs. I'd show him a thing or two about going postal! I made him write a thousand times, "Guns = violence and violence and the giving nature of the postal service don't mix."

That night, I massaged his little hand which had a bad case of writer's cramp while I sat down to watch the 5:00 PM news. I recoiled in horror and jumped across the room to change the channel. The newscasters were quicker than I and introduced their lead story, which blew a few hundred holes through the lesson I'd been trying to teach my son before I could reach the knob. He looked at me like I was the modern day version of Napoleon Bonaparte. I shrunk to the size of the dwarfed traitor when the anchorman said, "The Postal Service delivered another blow today as the Unibomber strikes again and causes more death and destruction."

Forget TV and Nintendo. Tomorrow I'd take them to the classic theater to see a golden oldie. Surely morals and respect for life would still be intact there. I was in luck, I thought, as I wrote down the schedule for the Wizard of Oz. Now this was a movie full of innocence, filmed with good old-fashioned lessons of character in mind. My sister-in-law and I packed the kids in the car and headed for the movie theater. After a pleasant two hours in a cool theater with no obscenities, violence, lack of morals, cruelty to animals, prejudice towards any race, and no disparaging or belittling remarks towards God, we stopped by my mother's.

"Grandma, Grandma! We just saw the coolest movie!" My sister-in-law and I looked at each other smugly being proud that we had managed to pull this moment off.

"Well, come sit down and tell me what it was all about."

"There was a really bad storm, and it threw animals and people and houses around."

"Yeah, yeah! And one feld on the bicked 'itch wif the booby lickers," her three year old kindly piped in.

"That's wicked witch with the ruby slippers," my sister-in-law sheepishly tried to correct but was drowned out by the excitement of the continuing plot.

Another nephew offered, "And they were trying to kill the evil monkeys with wings because they wanted to steal her shoes."

I changed tack. "Tell her about the little people, Mitch."

"Oh yeah, and there were these little people that they colored and put in really stupid-looking clothes and made them march on a road that either got them dizzy or led them into the forest where they'd be eaten by lions and tigers and bears."

"Oh, I see," my mother looked at us quizzically as we shriveled into the couch.

"And what else?"

"There was this old guy who turned out to be a big liar until he got caught and then had to pay restitution by doing community service and helping out the cowardly lion, the heartless tin man, the jittery scarecrow, and Dorothy. It was so cool!"

"What was this movie called?" Mom asked appearing a little confused.

My three-year-old nephew looked quite stoic and all too serious as he said with authority, "The Liver of God."

My mother looked at him completely stupefied, verbally and mentally left without a single response. I leaned over to my sister-in-law and whispered, "I think you ought to have his hearing checked and *soon*!"

It was Halloween time again and I approached my sons with non-violent ideas for Halloween costumes. I was thrilled when Mitchell said he wanted to return to a gentler time and be a positive role model this year. Maybe all these years of teaching had not been for naught.

He brought me his old postman uniform and I helped him untack the pants and unhem the shirt. The morning of his elementary school parade, I kissed him on the cheek, straightened his collar and smoothed his postal service patch before handing him his backpack and canvas bag. I then raced up the stairs so I could get ready before heading over to the school.

I had my camcorder on standby ready to video my smiling little postman when my neighbor elbowed me while laughing at the creativity of Mitch's disguise for the year. I couldn't see his smile. It was hidden under a medical face mask and his hands were covered by latex gloves that were holding a contaminated letter straight out in front of him as far as he could reach. What topped it all off, though, was the sign he had so meticulously written in big black letters to hang around his neck.

It said, "Through rain or sleet, sunshine, snow, and even anthrax too, no matter what, we gladly deliver to you!"

Even though he's really good at tuning me out day after day, at least I have the comfort of knowing that if I ever need to teach him an important and invaluable lesson, I can just put it on the evening news. I'm absolutely sure it'll make an impact then.

Life Lesson Number Fifteen:

☙❧

Appreciate your mother. For better or worse, you wouldn't be here today without her.

Come One, Come All

I stood there with my mouth wide open gaping at the TV. "It's the toughest job you'll ever love. Join the Peace Corps." Yeah, right. They obviously had never tried motherhood. I had honestly thought that was my motto.

M-O-T-H-E-R-H-O-O-D. Go ahead, say it once or twice. Despite what some would think otherwise, it's not a four letter word. In my opinion it kinda rolls off the tip of your tongue like the strained green beans your infant son just threw at you. And just like the green beans, you can't help but try just a little. Then you're hooked (on motherhood not the green beans).

The only problem with motherhood is that it's not looked at as a real job. Take every standardized printed form out there as an example. Under the "your name" line, it always asks for an "occupation" and a work number. The dictionary lists occupation as "Occupying or being occupied; specifically the seizure and control of a country or an area by military forces. Or that which chiefly engages one's time; one's trade, profession, or business.

I guess the seizure and control part could be fit into the realms of motherhood especially when talking about a teenage

82

son's room. I've had to seize their territories through what could be considered militant methods when the smell knocked me back out the room as I opened the door. I would even have to say that it takes a finely tuned strategist to mount the kind of search and rescue effort it took to isolate the stench. The sad truth is that most people don't think of motherhood as a trade, profession, or a business.

They should. I'm good at trades.

I trade kids with my neighbor when lugging a fifty-pound child around, who just wants to go home and watch *Rugrats* while eating a peanut butter and honey sandwich, is too laborious.

I profess to love my family and even do many time consuming and monotonous things around the house to show them how much I care but I'm quite certain that none of these qualify as a profession.

And business sense? I've got it. It takes a lot of financial savvy to run a home on a third of what is budgeted and extend a week's worth of groceries bought in May into September.

It takes real negotiating skills to bargain with a five-year-old when he's scared of the dark and wants to take over your bed by sleeping sideways because there are monsters under his.

It takes a finely tuned sales pitch to get an eleven-year-old to believe that wearing nameless plain blue jeans is just as hip, trendy, and style setting as wearing the overpriced chartreuse cargo pants with sparkle snaps that everyone else and their matching dogs are wearing.

It takes quick thinking to throw the best party of the year when twenty eight kindergartners show up to your son's birthday party instead of just the five you invited because he's since spoken to everyone in his class and all of them are now considered his very best friend.

It takes pluck to walk into a second grade class to hand your son his forgotten lunch money and pretend to know what you're doing as the teacher entrusts you with the keys to her filing system and the maps to all the fire escape routes as she steps out for a moment, which turns into what seems like three weeks of Sundays just because you paid your PTA dues.

And it really takes a knack of accentuating the positive when you declare in a loud proud voice that you've learned so much while staying at home with your children.

The top three on my list of Harvard moments:

1. I've learned how to dance the rumba by watching some large Muppet that lives in a big, blue house, which is decorated better and is fanatically cleaner than my own.
2. I've gotten back to the pure and simple pleasures in life by virtually walking under sunny skies on a pretend street with friendly repair people, grocers and fuzzy lovable monsters that I never seem lucky enough to have inhabit my home at three in the morning even though bedtime stories about them are pounded into my five-year-old's head.
3. This one's been a real coup! I've learned to appreciate the good in those fat little pear-shaped creatures that talk in gurgles and coos and think that television is so wonderful, they've evolved to include one as a standard part of their anatomy, so as to render them unable to wear clothes.

Every day I am using nursing skills, teaching skills, psychotherapy skills, business skills, chef skills, maid skills, militant sergeant skills, dry cleaning skills, decorating skills, gardening skills, coaching skills, creative skills, accounting skills, purchasing skills and I am forced to do it all without much help or sleep. I am Martha Stewart, Joan of Arc, Lee Iacocca, Vince Lombardi, and Mother Teresa rolled into one. But I have no formal occupation although being a mom occupies ALL of my time.

Thus, after seeing the Peace Corps commercial, I began my quest for a respectable title and a motto which would draw the masses into motherhood's sorority. A new phylum, a growing social class! We may be an exceptionally archaic breed, but we're still a proud one. Even Oprah thinks we're OK. I mean that's like God saying you're forgiven of everything rotten you've ever done in this life and the next.

I picked up my pen and paper and began to brainstorm. What words epitomized those few of us still left at home, feeling fulfillment in washing everyone's dirty socks? I wrote, "We're the few, we're the proud," before a flashing sword held in the hands of a *really* young looking pubescent in a blue suit with dazzling silver buttons appeared on my screen. He reminded me of my brother when he was six.

Another good one taken.

"Be all you can be" had potential but it was nabbed a couple of years back by the army. I was beginning to wonder why all the mottos that said something noble and challenging were already taken by organizations that ran through knee-deep mud and cleaned their guns for fun. I switched directions.

I was in the kitchen again preparing dinner for the second decade in a row and thought about "finger lickin' good," but the Colonel probably wouldn't want to share.

I listened and looked and thought and perused for the perfect motto and came up dry. So I did the next best thing. I had a bowl of ice cream. It didn't facilitate a faster thought process, but it made me feel better and momentarily forget about my quest.

The next day, as I was filling out my sons' pink emergency info cards for school, I came across the occupation line. This time I would do myself justice. Domestic Engineer. No, been done before. Child rearing, habitat enhancing specialist. Umm . . . no. Seemed too long and like I was trying too hard. I settled for Professional Domestic Progenitor. I figured it fit. I was progenitive after all.

Finding the perfect motto to motherhood still had me stuck in a quagmire of turmoil, so I went to my sister-in-law's to gossip and eat strawberries. I had wanted to see if she had any ideas but we got sidetracked when her son ran over the cat on his tricycle.

After bandaging boo-boos and eating a few more strawberries, I realized that the family sized box of macaroni and cheese in my cupboard and my sons growling stomachs were calling. I got up to go.

That's when I saw it. I'm not sure if it was a fleck of mascara caught under my contact that made my eyes water or just the pure simple realization that there, on a plaque on her wall, was the entirety of my existence, the full sum of my feeling, *the* motto to motherhood.

It said, "RAISING KIDS IS LIKE BEING PECKED TO DEATH BY A DUCK."

Life Lesson Number Sixteen:

Make peace with imperfection, or insanity will become your new best friend.

Supermom: Reality or Urban Myth?

What is it about human nature that stipulates once a person has reached a plateau of achievement, it suddenly is not good enough and they want more? I was at that point. I was a mom, but I wanted to be something more! I wanted to leave an imprint upon the face of the world that would be meaningful for generations to come! Bottom line, I wanted kudos.

Not necessarily the monetary kind (I wouldn't, however, snub my nose at that) but anything, anything at all, that would give value to all the endless drudgery I plodded through every day. I wanted to be the best in my field of expertise, a pioneer to those future generations who would tromp within my spent footprints. I wanted to be the Supermom of our age.

Forms of validation were rather hard to come by in my household. They got lost somewhere between the supply and demand of clean underwear and the scum that kicked my fanny in the shower stall. Appeasement through material gratification went out the door every morning when the kids and my husband fleeced me of the money I'd saved from rebates and clipping coupons. I couldn't hold as sacred or keep nice anything I'd managed to procure through covert operations for myself. (How they found the Nike anklets without holes in the back of my second drawer under a row of sea foam green socks with eyelet lace from 1982 and behind the cellophane from my last package of pantyhose is still a mystery to me.)

I'm not sure why, but I just wasn't finding the gratification I needed while running my paces in the House Spouse Olympics everyday.

I had mastered the Vacuum Tug-and-Pull. The Panasonic almost had me the day it lunged under the bed and snagged a pair of Mitch's boxers. It almost had them completely shredded and engulfed within its type U bag belly, but I was quicker and more agile. I threw it to the floor, capturing it in a straddle hold, and ripped the shorts back out of the clutches of its whirlwind bristle brush. There was no one there to applaud me after winning the dual over boxer death but the dust bunnies lurking under the dresser.

I had placed well in the Furniture Squat Thrust. I am still marveling at the fact that an 80 pound child can wiggle a 396 pound captain bunk set several inches out from the wall, creating a gap, which turns into a hazardous waste dump. It had taken plenty of training to master this field, but I managed it with the aid of a sturdy toy box placed strategically between my back and the wall. My knee brace also came in handy.

Then there was my favorite physical event, the one that surpassed all in the areas of stamina, agility, and patience—the Phone Ring Relay. This began with the first telephone ring at which point I would leap over a bed, hurdle three pairs of roller blades in the upper hall, fly down seventeen stairs to the next level, hop deftly through a field of ninety-three little metal cars at the bottom, avoid the snare of the vacuum cord, spin around the refrigerator door, belly slide over the cabinet while doing a leap roll to the telephone stand, all before the fourth ring when voice mail would curtail my success and pick up. My sons always upped the ante and made the competition stiffer by prepping the field and hiding the cordless hand unit so a race to the base was a must. I would stare at the caller ID box and tag it in disgust, "You're it." Another win to the phone line's unknown name, unknown number. I recaptured the title though when we got caught up on all the bills, and I had more people calling that I could actually pick up for instead of the mysterious unknowns.

There were contests of a mental sort too. I came in the top three of the Friday Scramble Fear Factor Challenge. Of course, I was only competing with the dog and a gang of Elmos, but that's beside the point. Every Friday I would buzz around getting the house in order for the weekend so I could relax. Don't laugh. I already said it was a challenge. This would invariably take me through three of the most nerve racking mental exercises conceivably designed for man. Strike that, make it designed for women—men would faint at the mere thoughts of such.

There was the Closet Contest, which in layman's terms was basically a timed face-off with my son's closet. I would thrust open the louvered doors and in less time than it took three growing boys to down a loaf of bread, a jar of peanut butter, and a quart of Great-grandma's fresh strawberry jam, I would have to locate, confiscate, and destroy the source of the offending stench. Mind you, though, that at times, there were booby traps. On numerous occasions, I had to dive for cover before the contents of the closet slammed down on me like Niagara Falls.

Second on my list was the Couch Championships. Without turning green or showing any form of weakness, like trembling knees or sweating palms, I would have to quickly plunge my hand into the dark recesses of the couch cushions and identify what was to stay (i.e. stuffing, springs), and what needed to go before either a.) it became a permanent fixture, or at the very least, a pungent form of fabric glue, b.) moved faster than I did, or c.) consumed my hand altogether. Only once did I ever back down and that was because the ants jumped the starting gun and had the bread crust into a pile of cinder before I could get to it.

Third, and my least favorite of the three, was the Laundry Survival Game. The game would begin when I pressed the spin cycle button on my washer at which time I'd dive for the hamper, choose a stained article of clothing, and in thirty seconds before the water shut off and the spin cycle began, identify the stain and figure out how to combat it, using the strongest combination of chemicals possible. This all had to be done without bleaching, discoloring or disintegrating the chosen article so it could endure and move onto the next round of wardrobe survival. (I might add that this game could also be played with the items in the fridge. However, the items chosen are of an indistinguishable nature and the chemicals chosen are to kill it, allowing you to survive the round.)

I had trained for an awful long time. I felt like I was now ready to jump to the next plane of motherhood and become a domestic diva, a princess of Pine Sol—a Supermom!

I enrolled in PTA and accepted a position on the board, volunteered as an art docent, taught the lessons for Junior Achievement, accepted a calling as the counselor for the eleven and under in Sunday School, was a den mom for the Wolves in Cub Scouts, juggled being a room mom in three classes, became a divisional director for youth soccer and took on managing my son's travel hockey team. All this was on top of maintaining the house; providing food and emotional support; keeping racks of clothes clean, mended, and up-to-date; and tutoring them through the first thirty-three years of life (that would be the combined years of my three sons).

My Expedition rebelled at the wear and tear by refusing to spit out refrigerated air when the thermometer reached 102. It calculatingly knew I couldn't take it in to be serviced because I couldn't be without wheels for a week. That was its ploy. With no refrigeration, it got a few more breaks than usual and was able to hang out in the cool garage while I slaved away in my home office.

The only nice part of never being home with my family was that I never had to hear them fight over the mundane and purely ridiculous things, like who got the frozen fluff in the bottom of the vanilla ice cream bucket that'd been defrosted one too many times or the proverbial war over whose turn it was to take out the garbage.

It was in the middle of doing all of this for my family that they decided to turn the tables on me by attaching themselves to my hip with a paternal umbilical cord in the form of a cell phone. A pager could be easily ignored and didn't come with cool games like Snake, Blackjack, or Mindblaster.

"Hey, Mom, how come you don't love us anymore?"

"What are you talking about? I'm bustin' my tail for you guys!"

"But you're never home. Oh, and Justin says it's my turn to take out the garbage, but I did it last week so I think it's Mitch's. What do you think?"

Mitch grabbed the phone and yelled into it using a decibel level that caused hearing loss for a week.

"Tell him, Mom, that you don't concur! I did it the week before."

I placed my Motorola on the passenger seat while it jumped and bounced from the sheer volume of the fight going on at home. I was glad I didn't have one of those digital camera units. The ugliness might have cracked the miniature LCD screen. When I really analyzed my expectations, I came to the conclusion that it really was too much to ask for peace at home while I was away when I had never quite figured out how to maintain it while I was there.

I had one night that week where I was actually able to watch the news at 10:00 PM instead of when it was rebroadcast at 2:00 AM.

"Join us for our human interest feature in ten minutes; the truth about the number one urban myth in America." I was hooked.

I sat through the next twenty-five minutes listening to how horrible this land was and the underlying message subconsciously being broadcast that only a dolt would even attempt to raise children in a world like this. Nonetheless, I strengthened my resolve to achieve where they were obviously daring no woman to tread. The broadcaster came back on announcing the story I'd been waiting for.

"On tonight's human interest feature, we will attack and dispel the notion that has haunted more Americans than the real conspiracy behind JFK's murder. We now go to Holly Houghton."

"Hi, Bruce. After much debate and research, we have determined with a 99.98 percent chance of accuracy that Supermom is indeed an urban myth."

So much for resolve.

Life Lesson Number Seventeen:

*If wisdom equals age and age is a state of mind, then it's
safe to assume that one can use wisdom as he gets older
to state his mind and never mind his mindless state
when having fun. Everyone expects old people to dress
oddly, have messy hair, and be opinionated anyway.*

Another One Bit the Dust

I, being of sound mind and . . . okay, so the body needed work. Who was I kidding? The mind needed work too, a *lot* of it. Let me rephrase. I, being of functioning mind and a body that I could still drag out of bed, thought that I had a pretty good grip on the age thing.

I had not inherited my mother's quirkiness and propensity to think that bust size, IQ, and income should all at *least* double one's age. She, despite the little telltale signs that gave her away (like the fact that her arms continued to flap even though she'd quit moving), fought with the officer typing up her license at the DMV for three and a half hours insisting that she was only twenty-nine. She relented by three years when her dentures fell out onto the counter during one rather heated interlude.

I had grown up listening to her banter about how she'd never succumb to age and all that went along with it. After spotting the Depends on sale one day, she flew to the other side of the store and performed Kegel exercises between the bakery department and vegetable isle, trying to ward off a hopeless future containing a malady every bit as bad as a grade 4 sarcoma called bladder failure.

She donned sunglasses that had lenses the size of #10 aluminum can lids and a scarf, which was long enough to mummify her upper torso, and drove forty miles away to a backwoods pharmacy where she could pick up stool softeners and Metamucil.

She also got into the sunless tan craze, but with her pale white skin and blue veins, she ended up looking like a zebra who'd been crisped during a nuclear holocaust. If that wasn't bad enough, she slathered it around her ankles trying to make it look even until she became the female counterpart to the old guy wearing sandals with dark socks and Bermuda shorts. The only problem was that her "socks" were fluorescent orange and clashed rather harshly with anything she put on.

I tried to get her to see how aging with grace is much more beautiful than the prospect of buns of steel under cottage cheese saddlebags and breasts that normally tickled her knees until she stuffed them into a Wonderbra. She wasn't buying. Attaching a label that read, "Not recommended for people as old as Noah or at the very least, those with pacemakers" to her Fanny Fantastic padded girdle didn't help either. I decided to take the straightforward approach.

"Mom, age is something to be proud of. You have more wisdom and poise."

"Yes, dear, the wisdom to hide the age and don't talk to me about Poise. I saw them on the aisle next to the Depends. Nasty little things they are! I can't believe you'd think they were something to be proud of!"

"I meant poise as in dignity and refinement."

"I'm no where near retirement!"

"Mom," I said.

"I can't afford to. We already have forty-three mortgages on the house. If anything happens to your father . . . You know, don't you, that I was serious about converting that really nice Tuff Shed in your backyard into housing. It's paid for, isn't it?"

"Yes, Mom, it's paid for. And I'll make sure that there are no mirrors and a scale that is permanently set at 112 pounds."

"I now know why you were always my favorite, or was that Bethie?"

"It was Rick, Mom."

"Did he promise me a Tuff Shed too? Which one has better coloring and more square footage? I might need a little more room for my thigh master you know. I saw Suzanne Sommers use it between her elbows to firm up her bust. If I could just firm mine a little more, I wouldn't have to use the wedges of foam under them."

"Mom, speaking of beauty enhancements, I'm concerned about the regimen you use every morning. I don't think it's good for your skin."

"The alpha hydroxy or the masks."

"The wood filler."

"Oh, I quit using that. I found that spackle filled in the cracks just as well and blended better with my skin tone before I put on my tanning cream."

It was hopeless. I'd have better luck trying to get Callista Flockheart to eat a hot fudge sundae.

I really and honestly thought that I'd left her hang-ups behind when I moved out of the house. I mean age is a state of mind. (So is psychosis, but that's another matter entirely.)

I didn't realize that some of the fears had subconsciously started to creep into my psyche as the cellulite and laugh lines became more prominent. I kept it well hidden until the day I drove by a local grocery store that was closing its doors and trying to clear out all of its items. That store had been there for more than forty years, I noted with a bit of nostalgia. Oh well, I thought. It's all part of change. I drove into the parking lot so I could look at the doors and read the marquis one more time.

It said, "Come on in! Over thirty specials until we close our doors."

I flipped a u-turn, screeched to a halt, parked the car and marched into the store demanding to see the manager. I harshly confronted the eighteen-ish, bow tied, acne-prone lad.

"I am ashamed of you! This has been an upstanding and valued establishment in our community for more decades than you and your mother in years combined have been alive. Folks from all walks of life and of all ages have gathered here before holidays, late on Saturdays, and on family nights for your twenty cent cones. And even though you have not been the cheapest, you have always been the favorite because you treated your patrons like family. So why on Earth would you go out in such a way that you would offend and rub the noses of those of us who just may be knocking on the AARP's door in our liniment of *old age*!"

He just stared at me like I was growing a rocker out my backside and a flabby flesh waddle where a youthful neckline had once been.

"Ma'am, what, pray tell, are you talking about?"

"Your marquis that says over-thirty specials. That is age discrimination in its worst form! And don't call me ma'am! I'll have you know that I am barely old enough to drive and buy my own Slurpees."

"Okay, mis-sy," he said, slowly and deliberately. "The marquis is referring to the thirty-four specials we have running during our close out. Might I also point out that one of them is Gerber Baby Foods, the stage one variety."

I wanted to throttle him for being smart with me, but age and embarrassment for lacking wisdom got the better of me.

"Oh," I said and wandered off sheepishly to the baby aisle and a quick detour through cosmetics where I picked up some anti-aging cream.

Justin came home from school and found me planted on the leather couch with a pad of paper, a pen, a personal CD player and headphones, several disks, a teeny jar of strained apples, and a baby spoon. It was the only utensil I could find that would fit in the jar.

"Hey, Mom, what're ya doin'?"

"Planning my future."

"Cool. A new house, a new car, a new baby?" He looked at the jar with curiosity.

"Not quite. My funeral. Thus far, I've narrowed it down to who will talk, who definitely shouldn't, where I'll be buried, and who I want to do the flower arrangements."

"Can't we plan my wedding first, or I know—my graduation from sixth grade!"

"Don't be so dramatic! That isn't even for another four days. I've also narrowed the music down to the song I would like to have playing in the background and for the processional. I want something that will epitomize my life and efforts here on this globe. Something sweet, simple, to the point, and lacking a ton of that syrupy, gaggy emotion. Something that is upbeat and has a good message. Here, what do you think?"

I put the earphones on his head and pressed the play button. He looked at me quizzically and then looked at the disk before breaking into laughter.

It said, "Another One Bites the Dust."

Life Lesson Number Eighteen:

❧❀❧

She who never gives up still has hope, and maybe someday that hope can reap miracles. This is true of any heavy burden, whether upon one's inner soul or upon one's inner thigh.

Willpower the Wimpy Way

After I had completed my funeral preparations, I realized that if I wanted to look good in the coffin I coveted, I'd better lose a couple of inches. Twenty to be exact. I, as of yet, had not been able to find an emerald green burial box with brass accents in a size 28. I took it as a sign that the good looking ones were not meant to look like piano crates nor did I want one that had to be altered with plywood creating a calico patchwork container in which to house my eternally slumbering body.

Thus began my quest to lose myself (twice over in fact) in the pursuit of a leaner, meaner (the kids say that can't possibly happen), fitter me. I sat down at the computer with three Krispy Kremes and a glass of milk and began my research. The dieting would begin tomorrow. Well, maybe on Monday. No one starts a diet on Wednesday.

I did a search on "diets" and came up with 2,040,004 hits. Hmmm . . . that was just a little too broad. No pun intended. I'd waste away while sitting at the keyboard and by the time I'd found the right diet, I'd be a size -4.

I added "that work" to narrow down my search. I came up with

591,004 hits. Still a bit too broad, so I scratched my head and then quickly typed "diets that really work." I got 206,004 hits. I began to wonder, if it was so blinkin' easy to find a diet that really worked, then how come half of America was broader than the back side of a barn? Maybe it was just a matter of finding one that was tailored to one's own specific needs and abilities. Patience, I just needed patience and another glass of milk.

Back to the keyboard. I typed "diets that really work and are quick." 62,704 hits. That was at least getting into the realm of plausibility. With a few more modifications I just might be able to sift through all the muck and find one tailored for me yet! I typed a little faster and watched the screen with the same type of childlike wonder that's expressed on Christmas morning. "Diets that really work and are quick and easy." 42,305 hits. We're still going in the right direction!

"Diets that really work and are quick and easy and last." Ding, ding, ding, and the number is . . . 21,905 hits. I was beginning to feel like Jerry Lewis during his Labor Day MS Telethon as the number board kept changing, giving positive feedback. I kept going. "Diets that really work and are quick and easy and last forever." 2,515 hits! Oh yeah! I was on a roll now! "Diets that really work and are quick and easy and last forever and ever" 148.

My pulse was racing and my heart was quivering. Had I known it was going to be so easy, I would've dieted years ago! I was acting like a compulsive gambler at the craps tables in Vegas needing a nightly fix. I brazenly typed in "diets that really work and are quick and easy and last forever and ever with chocolate."

I almost slapped my computer in frustration as it hummed and whirred trying to search the world's archives and stores of knowledge to bring me the one diet, my answer to happiness, *my personalized key to success!* Oh, oh, oh! Here it comes! The screen was loading . . .

I screamed with excitement and fervor, "Hand me the envelope please . . . and the winner is?" *Zero hits?* I knew it was too good to be true. I was so depressed I ate a peanut butter sandwich and French fries with cheese.

After licking my wounds (I had spilled ketchup on them), I picked up a book my mother had given me entitled "The Fat Thermostat" and began to study. The whole theory was that you needed to rev up your metabolism in order to lower the point at which your body needs to have extra stores. I was up for it if only I could find the gas pedal.

A friend suggested I try the cabbage diet. It seemed easy enough. Apparently you just ate a hunk of cabbage with every meal and the website even gave suggestions on how to prepare the cabbage in many exciting and tasty ways. Yeah, right. Maybe if you were a rabbit. I wiggled my nose, scratched my ear, and decided to try it. It kind of reminded me of the "bikini diet" I'd been forced to live on when I was fifteen and living with my great-grandmother. It wasn't fun, but the torture had been worth it. It was the best I'd ever looked. I'll expound so that any of you brave and adventurous enough who may want to try it, may.

Keep in mind that Great-grandma Dee was hard of hearing, hard of seeing, and would eat anything that didn't jump off the table. Easy food was a matter of practicality. But then again, who could blame her at ninety-seven? Matter of ease became even more necessary after her cataracts surgery when she had to wear patches and take thirteen microscopic pills, which required a looking glass to find them even with 20/20 vision. This is why I was living with her that summer.

She had a neighbor named Maude who loved to garden but had lost her green thumb sometime during WWII. That pretty much left her garden full of the only two plants that found her talents hospitable—morning glory and zucchini. She would bring Grandma a huge bag of zucchini every three days and pass them over like she was Jochebed placing baby Moses in his basket before sending him down river.

Grandma, who'd survived the Depression with more than one pair of stockings and a sixpence in her pocketbook, embraced the bag promising to cherish it. She dubbed it "bikini" (I told you she was hard of hearing).

She grated the bikini, seasoned it with cinnamon and milk,

and made oatmeal-like mush out of it for breakfast. We had bikini stew for lunch, and bikini burgers and orange Jell-O with julienned bikini for dinner. She made bikini smoothies for snacks and bikini cupcakes for desert. I think she used more bikini than flour that summer. Even if she had run out of flour, I'm sure she would've found a way to dehydrate and grind the bikini to replace the time-honored staple.

When I asked her if we could please have something other than bikini for a day she replied that the Good Lord had provided and it was our duty to use it and give thanks for the bounty. I didn't have the heart to tell her that "the bounty" didn't have one blessed thing to do with God being merciful. The stuff would multiply on its own in the vegetable bin.

I lost thirty-nine pounds that summer and was accused of being bulimic or anorexic. It had to have been anorexia. There is no way I'd want to purge and taste that stuff twice.

I did, in all fairness, reap some benefits from the experience. I have all of the material to finish my next writing project: "101 Ways to Enhance Food with Zucchini and Stretch Your Dollar." It'll be a big seller in Utah, where there's a large population who plant zucchini every summer.

I tried the cabbage diet for two days and then found out how it worked. The gas and smell one emitted necessitated managers of all food establishments to exercise their right to refuse service. One gentleman spelled it out quite nicely as he explained that he was mildly concerned that the other customers might run out the emergency exit in a rush to escape the odorous stench. He hadn't wanted anyone hurt by rioting. Safety reasons, you understand. One restaurant, though, offered to put me in their smoking section. Everyone back there already had their olfactory senses dulled by now anyway.

After having spent thousands on Jenny Craig, NutriSystem, Weight Watchers, Slim Fast, the LA Weight Loss Program, and abstinence (I skipped Curves figuring I had enough of them already), I finally realized that I was out of control and decided to turn my power and cravings over to my higher power. I went to Overeaters Anonymous.

I introduced myself as Mrs. Anything with a Side of Sour Cream, gave a donation, accepted my big blue book and little brown book, and got a sponsor. I settled in with rapturous attentiveness just as my sponsor leaned over and whispered, "Just wait until the end of the meeting. That's the best part!"

At the end of the meeting, we stood in a circle and held hands while saying the serenity prayer, "God, give me the strength . . ."

I leaned over to my sponsor and said, "You're right. This really is the best part."

"Oh, this is good, but it isn't the best part." With that, our group leader closed the meeting and announced, "For those of you who don't want to go right home, we will be having a sponsor support meeting and meet-n-greet in the banquet room at Chuck-a-Rama."

Finally, a diet program I could stick with!

Life Lesson Number Nineteen:

Embrace your roots. Strong roots are what allow you to grow ever steadily heavenward while giving you the ability to bend with the elements of this world.

Aren't Sequoias a Dying Breed?

When Brad found out that I had planned my funeral, he concluded that either I had entirely *too* much time on my hands or that I was literally losing my marbles. I couldn't offer him any help. Either one, quite frankly was a best-case scenario.

"As much as I love the entertainment of watching you fall apart at the seams of adulthood and watching you sleep walk down Sesame Street, I think you need a little more in your life. Why don't you get a hobby?" Oh yeah, easy for him to say. The last time he said get a hobby, I got pregnant with Josh, and my world was dumped upside down into a pile of, well, you get the idea. I'm still recovering from that "hobby."

After checking to make sure I'd taken my birth control pill for the day, I called my Grandma. "Brad thinks I am wasting away into a world of Teletubbies, Fisher Price, and goldfish crackers. He told me to get a hobby. That really hurt! I think it was his nimble attempt at being kind while trying to enforce his need for me to get a life. Can you imagine the nerve? After all, I *am* the one who gave life to those three heathens he calls his sons, except of course when Justin got his "Hope of America Award" from the Kiwanis. Then he was mine.

"Grandma? . . . Grandma?"

"Huh? Oh, yes, dear. Sorry I was just reading my new issue of *Genealogy Today*. There's a great article on genealogy bringing fulfillment by finding links to the past. Now what is it that you were saying?"

"Nothing, Grandma, nothing."

"Did I ever tell you about meeting your Grandfather and the old house on 16th Street?"

"About a hundred times."

"We'd gone to serve the boys at a quaint little cantina when . . ." Maybe I could find fulfillment by finding my links to the past and while I was there, I could let Grandma hitch a ride back to the present.

Despite her frequent and brief lapses back to the early 1900s (well, maybe a little more than brief. Okay so she booked weekend packages back to the ancient days of yore), she was a pretty sharp old gal. After finding her wandering the streets in the rain because her carriage was late, the family felt it prudent to have her tested for Alzheimer's. The doctor started off with a series of questions testing her sense of the present.

"Maude, what day is it?"

"The day of my doctor appointment, of course!"

"But what day of the week is it?"

"The day after yesterday and the day before tomorrow." She grinned. She was good at word games. One might even say she was a master. She had to be. It'd been a matter of survival since she'd had five sons within six years. It was enough to make me crazy just thinking about it.

"Okay, Maude, let's go on to another game. I'm going to go through a series of words and then I want you to remember them for a later time at which point I will ask you to recall them. Are you ready?"

"Ready for what? Hah! Almost had you there. My short term memory is fine. Go ahead." He shook his head, made a note, and gave her the list of words to memorize.

"Today—Family—Squirrel—Nuts—Bicycle—Doctor—Sunny—Tuesday—Afternoons—and Three. You got that, Maude?" She blankly nodded. He then told her a story with several details that he quizzed her on afterwards. Her reply?

"I read more exciting primers to my children when they were two!" He made a note again on his clipboard and then handed her a pad of paper and asked her to write down as many of the words he'd given her earlier that she could possibly remember. She took the pad, and started to scribble furiously. She then handed him back the note pad so he could read it. Not saying a word or showing any sign of emotion at all, he handed the pad over to my uncle and let him read it. It said,

"I am here *today* because my *family* thinks that I am *nuts* and crazier than a *squirrel*, who thinks that he can ride a *bicycle,* but the only one who is *nuts* is this *doctor* for treating me like a numskull on this fine, *sunny Tuesday afternoon,* which is one of only *three* that I can play Bingo on."

My uncle snickered, and the doctor motioned for them to continue their conversation out in the hall where she couldn't over hear.

"I think your mother suffers from mild dementia that is at its worst at night. We refer to it as 'Sun Downer's Syndrome.' That and an extremely overactive imagination."

"I heard that," she called from the examination room.

There was no getting around it, Maude had spunk. I wondered if any of my other relatives had as much pluck. I enrolled in a genealogy class that advertised the title "Discovering Your Family Roots." The teacher promised that through the course, we would learn how to dig up our roots and discover if they blossomed into a bonsai or a sequoia. Either way he said, we could be proud of our efforts and our heritage.

I learned how to use the pedigree software (does anyone else find it bothersome that our family roots are related to dog food?), track down civil and military records, read microfiche (What is it with the ties to human ancestry and animals?) and chart it all out on a family record sheet. The teacher, impressed with my efforts, offered to compile everything in the national database that'd already been done on my family.

Two weeks later, he excitedly handed me a stack six inches tall of computer printouts and a pedigree chart that was three by sixteen feet. "Your grandmother has been a very busy lady. Looks like you have the seedlings of a sequoia there."

"Sir, I appreciate the compliment and all," I said as I stared at the stacks of paper and the industrial strength paper tube he'd given me, "but I was thinking my family tree was beginning to resemble something a little more appropriate like maybe, uh, a creeping phlox." He laughed, patted my shoulder, turned on his heel, and walked away. I looked at the stack again. My family could've saved a redwood forest instead of bred one.

There were some interesting characters like the bearded white guy from Virginia. He'd been a war hero or something along those lines. I think his name was Lee. Robbie Lee, Rob E. Lee, Robert, anyway . . . it was something like that.

Then there was Pocahontas. That was a real find. Apparently, Geronimo really had seen a bit of Indian blood in me. I pulled out my pocket mirror and searched my eyes, bone structure, and jaw line. I still wasn't sure where, but my lineage said so even if it was only by 1/24.

Her name had been changed to Rebecca when she converted to Christianity after marrying her husband, John Rolfe, in England. I was quite excited to pass this tidbit of information on to my family. I pulled out my cell phone and quickly dialed. "Does this mean I can get a bow and arrow for Christmas?" asked Josh hopefully.

Justin and Mitch wanted to know if it meant VIP passes to Disneyland and a discount on the soundtrack and the animated movie. I guess this family tie hadn't quite made the impact on them that it had on me.

As I was returning home from class that evening, I heard my son out back telling his friends all about Pocahontas. So he had listened! I was proud of him for taking an interest in his heritage and even more pleased that I had finally found a hobby that enriched the lives of my children as well as myself. That's when I heard him exclaim, "And you know the best thing about her?" I waited as I too was wondering what stood out in the mind of a precocious third grader as her most noble achievement. "She was a movie star!"

"Well, if I can't make an impression on the lives of my sons, then at least Disney can," I huffed, and walked up the back steps and into the house where I threw my genealogy records into the corner by my computer desk. I'd get back to them at a time when they weren't quite so overwhelming. It would be a *long* time before that happened.

The next hobby I decided to try my hand at was cross-stitch. I found it challenging trying to decipher 457 microscopic symbols on a pattern in order to place them onto a grid with squares the size of a pin head. It took a few weeks and a gallon of antiseptic because I'd pricked my fingers so much, but I got the hang of it and started into a cross-stitch frenzy.

I stitched bibs and rags and every completed pattern handed down to me by a fellow stitcher, and yes, that did include the seventy-eight prancing pink bears that ultimately ended up in Josh's room. (Brad insists that this is part of the problem with his over-compensation and desire to assert himself as a dominant male force.) I stitched every family member's profile and even did a dandy little number on Mitch's head when he fell and split it. He looked like Frankenstein for a few days but the wound healed nicely thanks to my superior stitching. My family finally put their feet down though, and limited my projects to anything that could go on a wall when their undershirts started showing up with tiny kittens, hearts, and balloons stitched across the chests and sleeve hems.

I had just about run out of projects when my neighbor gave me a book with patterns for fourteen samplers. I was on the second to the last one—a nice little sampler with trees and squirrels that said, "Hug a tree, Have environmental responsibility"—when I finally decided that I'd had just about enough of this stitching marathon. Maybe it was time to get back to that pile of genealogy.

I looked at the tube teetering on top of the paper mounds gathering dust in the corner where I'd put them, what seemed like decades ago. It would have to be after I finished the last sampler though. I was determined to endure to the end. "Besides," I thought as I looked at the corner one more time and then back to my environmentally friendly project, "that pile would make any environmentalist roll over in his biodegradable grave."

Putting down my stretching ring and needle, I turned to the last page of my pattern book and started analyzing the symbols, trying to figure out where to start stitching tomorrow. That is when I knew without a doubt that God must have a sense of humor. It spelled out the words,

"My family can go on forever."

"Amen to that," I said, picking up my needle and ring.

Life Lesson Number Twenty:

Inevitably you will face your biggest demons in life. Just remember that dragons are slayable. God knows this and wants you to know it too. You gain strength by not only gaining ground but also by merely swinging the sword.

Toddler–864, Mom–0

When our little house finally succumbed to the noise level and rowdiness of three very healthy boys, we finally took pity on the foundation and cross beams, which seemed to constantly be screaming uncle, and moved into a house which was big enough that the dog had her own room.

That was a bone of contention for me.

It wasn't that she had her own living space, but the fact that we had her at all. I sincerely believed that my American dream was already complete with the white picket fence unencumbered by a barking fur beast. I tried to deal. I demanded that before my sons got a dog, they'd have to prove they could care for the other animals already living in the house.

"But Mom, there are no other animals living in the house," Josh bemoaned.

"Unless she's talking about you," Justin fired back.

"Maaaaybe she is," bleated Mitch.

I could see I was clearly losing this battle when Brad barked, "That was rrr-uff. How 'bout a moooovie night?"

"What have I done in a former life to deserve such mocking? What? Were you raised in a barn? You're all full of bull—,"

"Shnikees," Mitch howled as I used a dish towel to whip them.

"Besides you four animals, there are dust bunnies living amongst us. You can keep Mother happy by taking care of them with a broom and a dusting wand." I may have lost the war, but I was going to at least win a battle or two.

A new house is wonderful, but after a while, the pocketbook (if not the husband) pleads and begs for mercy and an extended rest. I turned a deaf ear. I was into a remodeling groove, stripping wallpaper, adding decorative moldings, painting, papering, carpeting, reupholstering, and rocking the fireplace. Although Brad's prayers for pity fell on my deaf ears, God heard him and sent me to the bathroom puking every time I smelled strong chemicals or peanut butter, and it happened when every project was only halfway to completion. Only pregnancy could make me feel this lousy. Here's the kicker though—it was with twins.

I got to know every crevice, crack, and water portal in my toilet bowl better than the Tidy Bowl Man ever could have. I was swollen, lifeless, miserable, and cursing fate and my husband, while lying on my back and staring at the ceiling, expending as little energy as possible. I needed to be conservative because even wiggling my toes caused my behemoth body to sweat in the balmy 109 degree weather, so that I shriveled quicker than a snowman in a hothouse. The swamp cooler wasn't working to boot.

Josh came in and sat on the edge of my bed and patted my enormous belly protruding upwards towards the ceiling.

"Is it true, Mom, that if we have as much faith as a mustard seed, we can move mountains?"

"Who told you that?"

"My Sunday School teacher."

"Then it must be true—yes, it's true. What is the point of this discussion?"

"Just wondering." He scrunched up his eyes, concentrated until he turned purple, and looked like he was about to pass out.

"What on earth are you doing?"

"Using my faith to move a mountain so you'll go make me lunch." I rolled my eyes, groaned, and waddled on down to the kitchen. Couldn't the kid just quit eating for a few lousy months?

My burgeoning belly also brought a gaggle of questions from my inquisitive son. This quizzical vein eventually evolved into a rather delicate conversation about the process of making a baby. I'd barely mentioned eggs being in the mother when he snapped his jaw shut, gave me a searing look of hatred, and stormed out. "Well, that was peculiar. What did I say?"

For days, he avoided my gaze, wouldn't speak to me, and spread nasty and heinous rumors through the PTA and the Teacher's Union that I was a blood sucking carnivorous fiend. I couldn't stand it anymore! If I'd wanted this much hatred thrown in my direction, I would've gone into politics. I called in a professional mediator, wanting to resolve the matter once and for all.

"Josh, I know you are mad at me over something. I can't, however, figure it out for the life of me. What is eating you? Throw me a bone here, kid, so we can end the animosity."

He slammed his fist on the table and pointed a finger at my nose. "You're horrible! You just love to rub it in my face don't you?"

The mediator broke in. "Let it out, Josh. Tell your mother what is anguishing you so we can then start the process of healing."

"Fine." He burst into tears and spilled the reason for his angst. "You told me that all babies come from eggs that are inside of mommies. Well, the way I see it, the only way an egg gets inside of you is when you boil it, crack it, and eat it. So it goes to figure that you ate me. And I thought you loved me! How could you do such awful things to a sweet little kid like me?" He then buried his head in his hands as uncontrollable sobs racked his small body.

I stared at him completely dumbfounded before I burst out laughing.

He lifted his head, folded his arms, pouted, and then glared at me with the same disdain as a vegan sizing up a Texas cattle rancher. I just laughed harder until tears poured down my cheeks and pointed at him. "You . . . ha ha ha . . . .just crack . . . ha ha ha . . . me up! No pun intended." I then rolled off the chair onto my back not even caring about trying to keep a decorum of seriousness about me.

The mediator leaned over to Josh and whispered, "I could get you a good divorce lawyer, pro bono, for this one."

A month later, Maison joined our family. His sister Emily did not make it, and laughter, for a while, was a rarity. I ached deeply at the emptiness in one of my arms and even more so for the hole that had been left in my heart. Well-intentioned people tried to ease my pain by reminding me that I miraculously still had one healthy child (my son's chances at life had been given a paltry 30 percent), but that only added to my emptiness. Conceptually I knew they spoke the truth but emotionally I could only grieve for what was lost. Rational thinking has a tendency to fly out the window in times of extreme sadness, leaving nothing but a world bereft of anything but that tunnel of aching and emptiness.

I moved through my days in a haze of habit and ritual. It was a good thing my autopilot kicked in because the wrenching in my chest dictated for quite awhile how much or how little I could instantly process without constraint of time. Healing, ironically, became a matter of baby steps, both figuratively and in actuality. I held onto my son while finding a way to let my daughter go. He was my anchor because there were not many around me at the time who could really understand the implications of mourning one child while celebrating the life of another. The situation simply had not been in any of my friends' repertoires of life's experiences.

That made me feel even more alone.

I would hold him in my arms wrapping his tiny fingers around my pinky and smile while crying. I watched his milestones and wondered where she would've been in comparison. Would she have walked first, talked first, said "Momma" first or been a step behind? Would she have been more studious or full of mischief? Most of all I wondered if she would've followed in my footsteps hugging her babies and whispering words of encouragement and motherly love

112

in their little ears. I tried hard not to entangle the existence of the two but every once in a while, I would look into Maison's eyes and see a part of her, a part I had lost and couldn't ever replace.

I was so grateful for my son and his will to hold onto life but I needed the opportunity to mourn. I had to lay my daughter to rest before I could give him my full attention and be the mother he deserved. I also needed to do it without being made to feel guilty.

Maybe someday I would have the time, ability, or wisdom to figure out why she was not meant for this world or my arms. Until then, every day was a matter of survival and just getting through.

The day-to-day minutia eventually pulled my thoughts back from her grave along with the whisperings from on high that God indeed loved me and ached along with me. It was the sounds of life from my fourth son, however, that got me through the toughest of those times.

To this day, every year I place a Precious Moments angel on the top of my Christmas tree. I bought it almost two years after losing Emily. It took me that long to face a symbol which represented the emptiness in our home. I still shed tears as I place my angel amongst the braches of the tree rather than being able to nestle her in my arms. But on that eve when I first placed Emily's ornament, I was finally able to look around at my four sons and thank God for all he'd given me. I had begun the early stages of the healing process. I had to. I was marching head on into a huge storm, an urban tsunami of sorts, called the terrible twos.

With my fourth son, I began to notice, chart, and study his very distinct and unpredictable traits. Maybe it was because I had plodded well over the hills of youth and could afford a bit of patience or maybe it was because instinctively I knew he was my last. Either way, I watched him with a fascination akin to a Wall Street moguls in a bear market.

I was impressed with his intuition and quick learning. His tenacity and desire boggled my mind. But it was his energy that completely knocked my socks off. If I could only have tapped into it, I could've solved America's energy problems and kissed the Middle

East off forever. What thoroughly amazed and confounded me, though, is that he was able to manage all of this in between his seven showers a day.

Tell me what it is about men that allows them to hold onto a football in all foul and undesirable conditions such as rain, hail, or sleet with little more than slippery leather and a few strings for grip and yet, the moment you ask them to hold a baby, they run for cover and feign incompetence at holding an object so small?

That, in a nutshell, is why Maison began the ritual of showering with Mommy at a very young age. It was convenient, quick, and soaped two birds with one puff.

As he hit his toddler years, the sound of shower streams brought him running from any far corner of the world. It didn't matter if he'd already showered three, four, or even six times already, he was always up for one more.

I'm not sure how he did it. I would merely think that is was time to shower, and he'd show up without a diaper, and baring tubes of tub paint in one hand and a rubber ducky in the other. Just once I wanted to outwit his shower ESP and enjoy the water stream and shower gel by myself.

There was one night I couldn't sleep, so at four in the morning I decided to take a solo shower. One minute fifteen seconds into it, he came trotting in crying, "Bad dweem, bad dweem." Yeah, I'm sure. He'd probably woken up with night sweats and a sense of terror because I was showering without him.

He was the most ritualistic toddler I'd ever seen! Everything had to be done a certain way! "I wonder where he gets it from," I mused as I watched him comb his hair, put on deodorant (someday I'll have to teach him to take the cap off), pretend to shave (he can leave the cap on for a while with this one), brush his teeth, and poke his eye out with an index finger covered in contact cleaning solution.

The fact that he screamed afterwards because it burned like heck never dissuaded him. It was part of the post-shower ritual.

I would turn on the water so he could flush his eyes to which he'd scream and say, "Me doed it!" He'd then blindly grope for the turn on valves until he could rinse in water that didn't either scald him or freeze his fingers off.

I would try to help him out, but he was sure he knew how to do everything on his own. At times I thought I should just turn over my laptop. He'd make a fortune writing how-to manuals. I was fairly sure sales would go down though when someone finally snatched a glimpse of the author, wearing a winter boot, a sandal, a floral Hawaiian print shirt upside down, and pants with stripes on backwards.

I was watching all four boys out front engaging in various acts of mischief one day when I was forced to ponder the ironies and variety of the "no-knows" in their lives. The homonyms circled round and round until I had to step in and peacefully try to settle their quibbling. I should have stayed out of it. I could've avoided a trip to Josh's doctor, the emergency room, and our own bad spoof of the Brady Bunch. Let me explain.

Josh was shooting a street hockey ball into his hockey net. It hit the garage, and bounced back into the street. Maison high tailed after it to which Justin screamed, "Maison, NO! NO!" and ran after him, plucking him off the curb before he could head out into the street.

Mitch yelled at Justin saying, "Don't yell at him. He knows."

Maison, in his ever sweet and annoyingly helpful voice, started screaming and flailing his extremities. "Me know! Me know!"

Justin set him down and said, "No, he doesn't," to which Maison gave him a good swift kick in the shin and ran off in the opposite direction.

Josh hooted and wound up for a slap shot while chiding, "Mitch told you he knows."

Justin rubbed his shin and mumbled, "I know, you dimwit, I know."

Mitch countered, "Do you know, Justin, that 84.3 percent of the world's population thinks that redheads with acne problems and a propensity to be know-it-alls are extremely unattractive? That should make it hard for you to find a date when you turn sixteen."

I watched Mitch, with Justin on his heels, fly past the window and let out a blood curdling whoop. I stomped out the door in a futile effort to mask the mayhem before we embarrassed ourselves in front of the neighbors and turned to Josh who was the only one left in the yard.

"Who started the fighting?"

He looked at me innocently, shrugged his shoulders, and hit the ball again. "I don't know."

The ball went wide and headed straight for the middle of my face. Josh shuddered as he heard the crunch, and I cradled my nose and loudly whimpered, "Ow! Ow . . . ow, my nose . . . owwweeee . . . my nose! How could you do that, you little creep!"

As I was heading in to find an ice pack that would help control the flow of blood, I asked my three boys (two of whom had returned from their chase at the sound of my hollering), "Where is Maison?"

In unison, they all shrugged and said, "Who knows?"

Forget about the neighbors. I yelled at the top of my lungs, "Maison, commmme heeeerre, right noooon!"

I heard a faint little voice coming from the neighbor's yard. "No, no, NO! I play wif my fend." I'm convinced that if Eve had really known what she was in for with her sons, the human race would be dead.

At least supervising Maison and his friend, Carter, made me feel useful. I had to be or the house would come crashing down on their heads.

It was interesting watching their two-year-old battles of will. In an effort to encourage nice playtime and a sense of cooperation, I plopped down on the carpet with poster board and a marker. I figured they'd be more amicable to rules if they felt like they'd had a hand in penning them.

"Boys, we are going to make some rules for playtime. Do you know what rules are?"

Maison burst out, "No, no, Maison. No, do that."

They both jumped up, and holding hands, jumped around in a circle, yelling in shrill two-year-old voices, "NO . . . NO . . . NO . . ."

I rolled my eyes and muttered, "I'm glad we have the concept of rules down. Boys, *boys*. BOYS! Can we please quit jumping and acting like monkeys?"

I shouldn't have mentioned monkeys because they then ran to the bookshelf and got the book on monkeys for me to read, and then the one on birds, and then another on zebras until we had read all the books in his alphabet zoo series. They, of course, had to act out each animal, complete with actions, sounds, and varying degrees of spittle. When we finished up with water buffalo (there was *a lot* of spittle involved in this role-play), I got up and fell back into the rocking chair exhausted.

After studying them for a couple of hours, I wrote my own rules, calling it the "toddler's tenet." It fit the mode of two-year-old play better than anything I had ever previously seen. It read:

1. If it's in my room, it's mine.
2. If I looked at it first, it's mine.
3. If you touched it first but I want it, it's mine.
4. If it's on the floor and I step over it getting to something else, but you decide that you want to play with it, it's mine.
5. If I played with it and then threw it aside so I could grab what you had and then you wanted what I had, it's mine.
6. If I broke it four and a half days ago, and I shoved it under my bed because it wasn't good enough for me to play with any more and you found it and think it's interesting, it's mine.
7. I eat what I want when I want and that includes what's on your plate, because yours is better, even though mine is the same, and I also have the option of spitting the remnants back onto your plate because I think it's yucky, even though you are crying and trying to spit back at me.
8. I will watch TV for two minutes, thirteen seconds after I have pitched a gargantuan fit and Mom has spent the last hour and a half fixing my favorite video tape to put it in the VCR for me

to watch, because she has four hours and fifty-five minutes of work to do before her dinner party tonight.

9.   I will scream in such a way that no one knows whether I am happy, hurt, stuck, or dying, and I will do this when someone is on the toilet with his pants around his ankles.

10. And finally, I will howl for forty-five minutes because its time for my friend to go home, and even though I acted like I wanted to kill him more than 7/8 of the day, he is my life, and I cannot bear to be without my friend.

One night, after a terribly exhausting day, after Maison and Carter had planted watermelon seeds on the basement carpet in dirt and manure they'd emptied from my container garden planters and hosed it down with the water bed kit they'd rigged to the basement bathroom sink, I said my prayers from a prone position on clean sheets that still smelled of fabric softener and thanked the Lord for being merciful in not allowing my daughter to stay.

In His infinite wisdom, He must've known that if He had, I'd have expired long before now and they'd both end up being motherless waifs. "Oh and, Lord, the next time we buy a new house or refinance our current one, please bless me with the acumen to accept that catchy little clause on flood insurance. I guess it does come in handy when having two-year-olds around."

Maybe it was because I was so exhausted and on the verge of hallucinations, but I could've sworn that in the whistling of the wind through the trees, I heard the faint sound of a little girl's voice saying, "Rest, Momma, peacefully rest." Either way, it gave me comfort and the will to get up and face the day again tomorrow.

Life Lesson Number Twenty-one:

A good marriage is like a casserole. Only those involved actually know what goes into it.

Hey There, Good Lookin'! Is Dinner Done Cookin'?

Kids are taxing. I take that back. To say they are taxing is like saying the Titanic was an incredibly sea-worthy little dinghy. They overwhelm you, completely blindside you, and suck the life right out of you. Not only on the physical, spiritual, and mental self, but on the part of you that still wants to be a person having romantic connections with anything other than dirty dishes and remotes. It's really sad when you can say that the alluring swish-swish sound of the dishwasher caressing your eardrums is the most exciting thing you've heard all day and that the remote has felt the touch of your hand more in the last three days than your husband has in the last six years. It was time for things to change.

When Brad came home that evening, I slinked around the corner, smiled, and cocked my head to one side.

"Hey there, good lookin'."

"You got something wrong with your neck?" he asked as he rummaged through the junk mail.

"How would you even know? You never even looked up from the Craftsman Tool sales circular from Sears."

"I saw your shadow off the side of the refrigerator when I took a drink out of the milk jug. What's for dinner?"

"I spent most of the day shaving—"

"It's about time."

"Ha ha, you smarty. I shaved, curled my hair, doted on my makeup after giving myself a facial, did my nails, and even gave myself a pedicure. Look." I pointed at my toes for him to see. He peeked over the Home Depot ad.

"What did you paint them with? A three-inch exterior trim paint brush?"

"So it's been a while. Listen, Big Boy, the kids didn't get here by us being schizophytes. There was a time when we had romance and reveled in each other's presence. I want some of that back. I want to remember why I love you."

"Is that possible?"

"I'm not sure . . . but I want to try." I smiled weakly. I took a couple of steps forward and snuggled up to his side. "Tell me you love me in that deep sexy voice of yours, Stud Muffin."

"All right. I love you, but I also love dinner before the news is over." His stomach growled for emphasis. I slapped it in mock protest before donning my apron.

After I'd cleaned up from dinner, vacuumed, swept the front porch, bribed the kids into doing their homework, bathed Maison, put them to bed, and weeded the back yard, I dragged myself up the stairs only to find flashes and smoke coming out from under our bedroom door. I was too tired to go back down and get the phone, so I yelled for Justin to call 911. I doubted he was asleep yet. "I think the house is on fire!"

Brad stuck his head out the door and coughed as smoke poured out around his head, making a macabre halo. "Cancel that call. It's just an experiment going on in here." He grabbed my wrist, pulling me into our room, and shoved me back into the lounge chair.

"You're in your bathrobe," I wheezed while fanning my face, "and what is that stench and this smoke?"

He ripped off his bathrobe and did a couple of wide swings with it over his head before launching it into what was supposed to be my lap. He dang near took my head off.

"Not anymore," he huskily countered. Brad started to prance around in a Philippine loincloth in the most ridiculous manner I'd ever seen. "It's incense and a smoke machine I borrowed from the Cantrell's. They only used it once and didn't need it anymore." I would like to say he then nimbly jumped up onto the dresser, but it took a bit of effort, even with the laundry hamper he'd turned over to use as a step stool.

He plugged in the strobe light he'd set up on the armoire and began dancing to Rod Stewart's "Do You Want My Body?" I grabbed a matchbook from the drawer in the nightstand, lit a match (I didn't have a Bic), and started to sway. Being inspired by my show of support, he did a split-legged jump off the dresser and ended up rolling into a heap, wincing in pain. I dropped the match, which had burned down to my fingers, and stomped on the charred sliver of cardboard. While sucking on my finger and thumb, I helped Brad to the edge of the bed.

"Now, Justin can call 911. I think I broke my ankle."

"He's asleep."

"Oh. Then maybe you can just scare me up an Ace bandage, an ice pack, and some ibuprofen."

"Do I dare ask why the Cantrell's didn't need their smoke machine any more?"

"Probably the same reason I now need to ask them if I can borrow their crutches."

"I would've loved to have seen their rendition." I chuckled under my breath as I went to fetch the first-aid supplies.

Since strenuous physical activity was out of the question for the next six to eight weeks, we decided to make our phone conversations throughout the day more "meaningful." When he could slip away for a moment, he'd call and whisper sweet nothings and every unfulfilled fantasy into the mouthpiece. It was the closest we could come to intimacy without the interruption of real life.

The phone rang one afternoon and I sprang to the jack. I cradled the receiver and stammered, because I was out of breath,

"Well, . . . helll . . . heellow (gasp) there. I've been . . . waiting for your call . . ."

There was silence before a deep and throaty voice said, "What are you wearing?" Wow! He was really into it today. Either that or he had a frog in his throat. Garnering a bit of competitiveness, I figured I'd play along and show him just who was better with words.

"Shall I detail it all out for you, Mr. Big Hunk?" With that I proceeded to outline some fantasy I'd once read in a romance novel. The gasps on the other end of the line just encouraged me to get more graphic as I imagined my husband straining to control urges to run out of the office and into my waiting arms at home (that is, of course, after I had arranged for Maison to go play at his friend's house for a few minutes).

The moment was broken when a completely unknown, squeaky, unnerved voice came through the line. "Lady, you've cured me. I'm resorting to 1-900 numbers from now on. They're a lot less sick than you lonely housewives, and you, I must say, top them all!"

My jaw dropped as I heard the click of disconnection. I walked to the caller ID box. "Please, let it say Brad's work, *please*, PLEASE?" It said *Unknown Name, Unknown Number.* The only comfort I had was in knowing that he wouldn't go to the police. He couldn't, unless he wanted to admit that he'd called me first.

When Brad did call (I verified that it was him by quizzing him on what he cleared every paycheck, his mother's maiden name, and the NHL Stanley Cup winners since 1962), I told him that maybe we ought to stop our phone game. It was getting dangerous.

"For whom?" he asked.

"For the obscene caller who just got an earful. I'm pretty sure we're going to get sued for his psychiatric care bills and compensatory damages for pain and suffering at the images I gave him. Oh, and put me in for ten dollars for the office pool. I bet I win 20 to 1 on this one."

As Brad and I lay in bed watching TV, out of the blue he chuckled and then chided, "So, play with any fun guys lately?"

I snorted and rolled over before snapping, "The only fungi I will be playing with from now on is that which is growing in the corner of the shower. I'll woo it into submission with my yellow latex gloves, stiff bristle brush, and X14."

"Oh, you wild thing, you!" he guffawed.

I fell asleep long before he'd quit laughing.

Life Lesson Number Twenty-two:

Life's tapestry is woven with some very dark colors. Ironically, it is not meant to veil one's countenance in defeat but to lift one up, revealing his character.

How Did the First Generation Ever Get the Starship Enterprise Off the Ground?

I'm thoroughly convinced that every generation can be assessed and pinpointed somewhere in time by their technological IQ.

Case in point—our grandparents' idea of a calculator was a man behind a desk with thick glasses, stacks of notepads, and an empty soup can filled with sharpened pencils. If he was a scientific calculator, he might have a chart of the elements pinned to the wall behind him while one specializing in algebraic equations would have a slide rule in his pocket and a protractor in his side drawer.

You knew this was the generation who'd lived through the depression because any gadget cost money, and nothing was cheaper than good old brain power. It was also a slower time where one could afford the luxury of spending three months doing what today's employees are expected to do in three hours.

I once got my grandmother an answering machine so that the family could leave messages and then call 911 if she didn't respond within a reasonable amount of time. I'd then given her daily two hour courses for a week on how to use it. I covered everything making sure she was completely comfortable with the machine. The next week I called and when neither she nor the answering machine picked up, I blazed over there in a panic. I found her out watering her flowers. When I asked her why her answering machine wasn't on, she replied that she hadn't liked the way it talked back to her.

"That thing was too cheeky, the way it tried to imitate everything I said, so I thumped it a good one with my cane, and it hasn't talked back since." I had obviously forgotten to teach her about the memo feature.

Our parents' ultimate goal is to "learn computer," the new universal language vital for survival and necessary for minimum functionality within the twenty-first century. They'd also like to be able to use and correlate the sixteen remotes that run a standard HDTV big screen, hooked up to the DVD player, CD player, and stereo system with THX surround sound, without losing what is left of their sense of pride. Dad once sequenced the remotes out of order, and the CD and DVD players concurrently spit out disks at him in protest. I don't even mention digital cameras, scanners, or photo quality printers. To do so would unnerve them to the point of catatonic technology psychosis.

We once signed Mom up for a class that taught Windows navigation, so she could eventually learn the basics of MS Word. The instructor refused to let her back into class after the first lesson unless someone accompanied her to the remaining classes.

"Where did you go wrong, Mom?"

"I think it was when he asked us to turn on our computers. Mine just beeped and whistled so I hit it with my shoe."

"Was the screen blank?"

"It was kind of staticky. When the TV does that, I hit it right on this little spot on the side panel with my shoe and it shapes right up. The instructor did tell us to boot up. Either way—boots or shoes—I figure you wear 'em both on your feet."

Brad ended up picking the short straw.

Week two, he had to ease her out of the classroom's rafters

when the instructor told her to grab the mouse. She later admitted sheepishly that she might've overreacted just a hair when rodents were mentioned.

He tackled the advanced capabilities of Word and Excel while she tried desperately to find the arrow that'd disappeared because her nervous jitter had caused it to fly to the edge of the monitor and then stay hidden in the blue cloudy vastness of her desktop picture. We all hoped she'd at least come out of the class with the confidence and knowledge that she'd accomplished something good, even if it was only learning where the power button was.

When the course was over, they'd both been presented with their completion certificates. Brad's had a nice little Microsoft seal, certifying him as an expert in several programs, while Mom's was a notice of incompletion with a handwritten note stapled to it that suggested she learn how to use an electric typewriter. The motherboard on her PC subsequently filed a restraining order if she ever set foot in that classroom again.

We are the generation who took phones on the go, conquered the world with handheld organizers, and began to understand the awesomeness of the World Wide Web. It is our children, however, who by age three are googling URLs that will hook them into Cookie Monster's personal email.

By age seven, they have figured out how to hook caller ID into the television, so they can decide whether or not they need to answer the phone while playing their Sega game on the top half of the set and watching *Rugrats* on the bottom of the screen.

By ten, they have learned how to reprogram their parent's phones with 109 different ring tones, text message anyone in the world, and redirect the space station using nothing more than a phone line, microchip and a keyboard, so they can get a good live digital feed for their fifth-grade science fair project.

I shuddered to think what middle school would bring. It was time to get them back to the basics, back to their humble beginnings, back to something of a more simple and archaic age. It was time to go see Grandpa and Grandma.

That was the day we found out that Grandpa, at age sixty, had cancer.

Suddenly, all the technological advances in the world were not enough. I'd already lost two grandfathers to this disease at early ages, and I was bound and determined not to lose him. Despite the many times I'd rolled my eyes at his antics, he'd always been one of my best friends, my mentor, my confidant, and teacher. He was my dad and my anchor.

The whole family dealt with it the best way they knew how—with passable (if not downright sketchy) faith, continual prayers, and some laughter. He'd not have it any other way. Dad wouldn't allow more than a couple of days to go by without a few good chuckles here and there.

Personally, however, I was crumbling. On top of everything else, this news had come at a time when I was already beginning to wonder if God hated me and had it out for everyone I had ever loved or cared about.

With 9/11 on top of the dot-com bust, every male member of my family had faced long periods of unemployment and even longer periods of uncertainty. What killed me the worst, though, was not the financial ramifications but the inability to make it all better for everyone. More than anything I longed to swoop in with my first aid kit full of life altering Band-Aids and soul healing salve. Lately, though, it seemed as if my Midas touch had headed south during this fiscal nuclear winter and was turning everything to either ashes or heaps of crap.

Dad had always taught me that even though God would challenge me, He'd also make sure that there were safety nets to keep me from falling. So how come it felt as if God had forgotten what my breaking point was and was letting the walls of emotional distress completely crush me. Watching my father's battle with cancer had left my chest feeling a bit too compressed as I felt the weight of the disease's impact on my family once again.

I lay awake at night as I visualized this man, who'd been my biggest critic and an even bigger champion as I waged the battles of my life. Living would never be the same if he were gone. I felt like a five-year-old, inwardly throwing tantrums, while the mature and respectable side of me squelched the screams longing to get out. My heart ached so badly at times, I felt like I was having a coronary. Hard as I tried, in moments of solitude I could not stop the tears that ran freely down.

If anyone asked how I was doing, I replied stoically that I was fine. I was too ashamed to let anyone know that this situation was getting the best of me. I figured it was far easier to live behind a wall of seclusion than to live in a glass house. If someone tried to peer into the windows of my soul, I simply shut the curtains.

It was Dad who finally saw through my isolation as I visited with him in the hospital keeping the conversations to small talk.

"It's a nice day out, blue skies and clear. You can see all the way to the airport."

He rubbed his bald head. "Clear. Kinda like my scalp. Well at least I don't have to worry about receding hairlines anymore. They've already receded so far they've gone up over the top of my head and down past my butt." He lifted his left leg with all the radiation tubes hanging out, making it look like a gigantic centipede, and plucked a hair from his clean sheets. "How'd I get so lucky to have only one by my bedside today? Those Samoans have nothing on our family."

"They most certainly do—they have a lot more hair," I said. I took the hair from him and dropped it onto the floor. "Look at the bright side. Uncle Fester and Telly Savalas are singing your praises since you make them look like GQ models by comparison." I rubbed his head as he laughed. "Besides, it'll grow back, and when it does, I figure you'll look like a Chia Pet with tresses the texture of Velcro. You look like you've been losing a bit of weight too."

"Yeah. With the aid of these fabulous chemo cocktails I've finally been able to drop those last pesky forty pounds I've been struggling with since 1981. And when your mother tries to chew my backside, I can laugh and tell her cancer already took multiple pounds of flesh." He cupped what was left after surgery of his right cheek and upper thigh.

"Nice." I grinned. "Hey, and how 'bout those drugs?"

"I think those are more for your entertainment. Your mother told me I named my urinal Lucky Lucy while under the influence of my last dosage."

"After Grandma? You always name things after her. The old station wagon, the sectional, your favorite armchair, the neighbor's dog, Taylor's middle name when you thought he was a girl. I think I would've personally named it Peter."

"Me too." He chuckled. "If I'd been coherent at the time. At least she stopped me when I grabbed it and thought it was a mug full of cream soda."

I shook my head in disgust at the thought of that one. "Hey, for a guy who loves nature and the big outdoors, the nice thing is that with the notoriously modest fashions provided in hospital wear, you won't be missing out on any full moons."

He laughed until he had to cradle his leg to keep from popping his stitches. A tear escaped from the corner of his eye. When I reached over to wipe it away, he grabbed my hand.

"You know, Stace, there are worse things out there than dying." That word poured over me like a cold shower.

"Like what?"

"Not living. Don't be so afraid of losing that you shut everything out and keep yourself from enjoying life."

Tears sprang quickly to my eyes. "Dad . . ."

"I know, Stace. But if you love me, live the way I've taught you to." I was uncontrollably sobbing by this point and couldn't say another word.

"There is one other good thing to all this radiation I've been receiving. In the dark I glow like a night light. The tips of my nose and knee caps light the way to the bathroom like the green lights on the airport runway. It makes it pretty easy to come in for a landing on the bathroom seat." My sobs turned into a mixture of choking from the phlegm, crying so hard, and sputtering through moments of lighthearted laughter.

"What's so funny?" I turned to see Mom standing behind me.

I got up and ushered her into the chair I'd been using. "Dad'll tell you. Besides, I need to get going." I kissed each of their cheeks and headed out the door. I turned back and watched her gently cradle his hand.

I looked at my mom and saw something I'd been remiss to ever see before. Or more accurately, maybe I just hadn't needed to see it before.

She'd been the woman I watched as a ten-year-old trying to corral the dog into the backyard before he could have an accident. When the dog ended up on the couch, avoiding the loony woman waving her arms in arcs and whooping at him, she hadn't skipped a beat. She fetched the vacuum, put it on the couch, and turned it on. The dog, who was more scared of the vacuum than the crazy lady, jumped off the couch onto her new carpet and urinated in fear.

I got a scrub brush and helped her until there wasn't a dribble left.

At twelve, I watched as she cried because a mother bird, who had built a nest in the air conditioning vent, had pushed her babies into taking their first shaky steps and watched as they had failed. She cried even harder when the mother bird pushed them to keep trying until the birds finally succeeded and flew away that fall.

That moment, for her, had defined the true nature of motherhood and selfless love—putting one's biggest fears aside for the betterment and ultimate joy of knowing that you've done your job and your children are succeeding on their own. Every fall since that day, as the kids returned to school, she would remember the birds and the role of a mother, and she would cry mixed tears of joy and sadness.

Back then, I had put my arm around her and told her I'd never be far away.

At thirteen, I watched her secretly act out a scene from "Beach Blanket Bingo" in her old blue polka dot bikini in front of her dresser mirror. I sat down on the edge of her bed and told her that she looked great for an older lady.

I watched as sadness mixed with a hint of wistfulness in her eyes as she came to grips with the disappearance of her youth.

At seventeen, I watched her with a bit of disdain as she sat at the table one Sunday afternoon looking at all six of us and said with the shock and utter amazement of someone who'd just won the ten million dollar lotto, "I'm a mother!"

I rolled my eyes and said, "Duuhhh." I figured she had become a birdbrain.

At nineteen, I'd fought with her because she'd tried to force her dreams for my wedding upon me. She'd put her foot down when I'd asked for a miniature waterfall under the cake with rose colored water matching the decorated fondant tiers. She said it made it look trashy. I ordered the fountain anyway, yelling at her and telling her to get out of my life. I was sure I completely understood why the baby birds had flown away never to return home again.

I did not see her cry that time but hoped that she had.

Throughout my twenties as I had my children, I watched her wring her hands and fret over my brothers and their choices in mates hoping that these young women would support them through their educations. She had wanted my brothers and their families to be able to live out their dreams. Education afforded better jobs and better jobs afforded dreams. Only when those diplomas were obtained could she rest peacefully, knowing that they'd be okay. And she had later fretted over Bethie's choice in a mate, hoping that he would give her the life my mother was sure Bethie deserved. She later told me that she had never needed to worry—all of our mates were the best things that could've ever happened to her children.

I finally understood why, when looking at my siblings through a mother's eyes, she had cried over the baby birds.

And now at thirty-seven, I was watching her at my father's bedside having patience, adding strength, and holding onto faith ,believing that all would be well. She was fighting for him with a determination that only someone in that situation could understand. I smiled as I headed around the corner. I knew I didn't need to be there to catch her if she fell. She was bravely moving forward into unchartered territory and handling it with the grace I wish I had.

But when I got home, I cried because somewhere in the back of my mind, I knew she had taught me to be the mother bird. At that time, however, I did not know how important those lessons at the hand of my qualified and magnificent teacher would be.

I learned something during those days. There is something far scarier than facing technological advances and everyday changes and that is facing the loss of the best parts within each of our lives. Those would be the ties that keep us firmly grounded in the things that really matter. They are the ones who make us cry and rejoice, make us angry, and that make us reach deep within ourselves to find the charity, compassion, and strength we never knew we had.

They are our loved ones. They are those we embrace and know as our families.

Life Lesson Number Twenty-three:

Life is like a roller coaster. You can scream every time you hit a bump or throw your hands up in the air and enjoy the ride.

Summertime Blues

I think that summer vacation was invented by some demented, jealous, lonely old spinster who couldn't have children of her own. I'm doubly convinced that she wanted to punish those of us crazy enough to have more than one of these little monsters through a series of tortures, which include constant fighting, laziness, and whining choruses of "there's nothing to doooo . . ."

I'm sure she'd be happy knowing that there have been more than a few summers when I would've gladly tracked her down and paid her my life's savings, if she'd just take them off my hands. She herself could then feel the all encompassing joy of castigation by children on summer vacation that are about as much fun to be with as a drill sergeant with OCD on cleaning day.

This summer was quickly shaping up to be one of those summers.

I was lamenting my lot in life when I heard from upstairs a blood curdling squeal that rivaled any screeching teapot. I raced to the source of the shrill sound, which brought me to the upstairs bathroom where Maison was standing naked with one of my hair clips chomping down on his privates. I had to giggle, but just a little, as he stuttered through sobs while droplets of water from his most recent shower dribbled down. Apparently he'd wanted to make his "outcropping" look pretty.

I retrieved my hair clip, looked at my son, and said, "Sweetie, there is a word that you should learn right now in order to avoid this kind of pain in the future. It is phallicism. It means worshipping yourself," I pointed to his boo-boo, "as the ultimate symbol of male generative power." He looked at me like I was speaking Greek.

"Never mind. You'll get it someday, and if you don't I'll just tell you the story of John Wayne Bobbit. Then you'll see how certain items and certain parts of the male physique don't mix."

I wrapped a towel around him, picked him up, and headed down the hall to fetch an outfit for him to wear. As I did so, I passed Justin's door.

"What was he crying about now?"

"He just tried to enhance his family jewels with a hair accessory."

"He did that last week too. I told him to knock it off. That kind of behavior would only lead to pain and misery."

I ruffled Mace's hair with his towel and chided him. "Are you suffering from that darn juvenile Alzheimer's again?" He nodded yes with an ear to ear grin before I turned back to Justin. "I thought you were going to clean your room.'

"Why would I do that?"

"So you can live in a clean environment where you can actually step on the floor without wondering if you're killing the vermin that live underneath all that clutter."

He rolled his eyes at least once for every year he'd been alive and flatly stated, "Very funny, mother. There are no vermin."

"And how would you know? You haven't seen through to carpeting in over two years." I hoisted Maison over onto my other hip as Justin did a three and a half with a double reversal with his eyes. "Impressive, my son! You might even have medaled in the eyeball Olympics with that one."

"Ha, ha, ha. I can't wait to tell my friends that one." He grabbed his left shoe with the tip of his toe and flipped it up unto his hands so he could slam dunk it into position before walking out the door.

"Where are you going?"

"To the elementary school. I have work. We have to scrub down all the walls, move the furniture, and scour all the bathrooms."

"Why? It's summer break."

"Because the district doesn't have the money to replace everything so we have to take care of it and keep it nice."

"Oh, I see. And who taught you this little tidbit of wise advice?" I looked at the cluttered cave he lived in once more and picked up a sock hanging off his doorknob.

"Scully, my boss."

"Then tell good old Scully to come on over here with his custodial crew and disperse some more of his pearls of wisdom and a gallon or two of pine cleaner. I'll up what the district is paying him by a dime."

Justin brushed passed me, rolling his eyes and exhaling so forcefully, it blew one of my earrings off. "Oh, and ask him if he'd like me to autograph that copy of *Things Your Mother Tried to Teach You but They Just Went in One Ear and Out the Other* for him. I'm glad he got some sound advice from it."

I'm pretty sure his eyeballs were doing flips all the way to school. Impressive when you realize that they were probably spinning against a head wind of thirty-two knots from all the exhaling that was happening as he thought repeatedly about what a geek he had for a mother.

After dressing Maison, I sat down in my rocker and tried to remember if we'd ever punished Mom and Dad this badly during summer break. I didn't have to reach too far back into the recesses of memory before stumbling upon a recollection of the water park we'd conned Dad into taking us to. There'd been a new attraction called the water roller-coaster, and we'd been dying to try it out.

We went on opening day and had ample time to study the ride's instructions and analyze everyone's technique. The object, apparently, was to go down one hill and gain enough momentum and lift to get you over the next hill. If you didn't get enough lift, you'd only make it halfway up and then slide back, rocking back and forth, in-between the two, like a human pendulum, until gravity forced you to the bottom where you'd then get off the track.

If one failed to reach the pinnacle of the second hill, a swarm of impatient hot-tempered and ill-mannered people, who'd been stuck in line, would stomp and groan, vibrating the whole structure. They would then hiss at the lame-o skidding to a stop and trying to disembark.

It was more humiliating than being caught with your skirt hiked up in the back of your panty hose or finding that you'd forgotten to zip your fly.

Bethie didn't make it. Tom didn't make it. Rick tried swimming up the backside of the hill with some really fancy aerial acrobatics but ultimately failed. Devon, however, made it by the skin on his teeth giving the rest of us a glimmer of hope.

I put my mat down and pushed off. Careful . . . remember control . . . gently lift the mat . . . up, up . . . a little more . . . and *yes!* I was *over!* I don't think I would've normally made it, but the saddlebags on my thighs, flattening out like shark fins, coupled with my oversized t-shirt, which inflated like a spinnaker, gave me an edge, tremendously aiding with aerodynamics and lift.

Dad was next. I need to insert here that he is a very competitive individual, who revels in the most miniscule and ridiculous forms of competition. He even once threw a party and printed up championship hats and shirts because he'd managed to beat my brother in a thumb wrestling contest, best of three.

He pushed off, ripping the edge of his mat up and leaning backwards, until he resembled a u-turn sign.

He got lift.

He got so much, in fact, that he flew over the top of the second hill, heading straight for the moon. Halfway down the front side, he managed a rather graceless free fall at the end of the track. He then continued skidding across the pool until he realized that if he didn't find a way to stop, he'd keep on going all the way to Toledo.

He bailed, landing in a choking, sputtering heap at the feet of a Bay Watch wannabe, who was holding a life saving water weenie and wearing a yellow tank top that was brighter than the sun.

"Hurry and step out of the pool, sir. Did you enjoy the ride?"

He looked at her from under the hand he was using to shield his eyes from the glare of her suit. He then grabbed his water mat and hollered loud enough that a frightened child over on the Kamikaze slide began to cry. "*Nice ride?* That thing outta be *outlawed*! Or at least come with a warning label for old geezers like me, who think they are still young enough to compete with snot-nosed kids who are a quarter their age!"

Okay, so maybe I deserved the penance summer break had to offer, but how come no one else seemed to be having as torturous a time and facing as much retribution as I? Surely the world was not filled with adults who had been perfect angels instead of rotten little snoots like me. Was it?

I grabbed the garbage and headed out to the can for the thirty-sixth time that week. The garbage had grown by leaps and bounds with the papers, wrappers, and boxes housing the food they devoured by the kiloton, and I wasn't in the mood to argue semantics and figure through algebraic calculations whose turn it was to take it out.

As the lid fell with a loud thud, I heard a weary and anxious voice coming from the window well of our neighbor's basement. I squatted down peering through the security bars they'd installed the summer before. "Al, is that you?"

"Oh, thank goodness you heard me! I've been stuck in this room with Carter for the last six hours while Mary and the other kids went shopping and to a movie."

"How'd you manage that?"

"I turned the doorknob around so Carter couldn't lock himself in the storage room again. He's done that a couple of times you know."

"Yeah, I know. He and Mace painted the shelves with peanut butter and stuck the whole wheat and garbanzo beans down the drain two months ago after they locked themselves in there for a couple of hours. We split the bill for the locksmith and the plumber."

"Oh sure, you'd remember that. Anyway, I came down to get some more jelly for lunch, and Carter turned the lock and shut the door when he followed me in. Will you come down and unlock it? I think the front screen is open. If not, just bust the front bedroom window. They gave us a frequent buyer pass at Harper's Door and Window last summer after Alan put a baseball through the back window, Kerry kicked a soccer ball through the Smith's sliding glass door, and Kylie put her curtain rod through her screen when she was trying to put polka dots on her valance."

"Sure, I'll be right down. Maybe afterwards you can come lock yourself in my padded room. It's where our storage room used to be. You can gather your bearings while I watch Carter and Maison for a bit."

"When did you do that?"

"I had it converted after they planted the watermelon patch and flooded the basement last year." He nodded in complete understanding.

It was nice to know I wasn't all alone in this summer full of parental punishment.

Life Lesson Number Twenty-four:

Learn to laugh and don't always be so dead serious.

Frankly Speaking

After Dad had been released from the hospital with a fair-to-good prognosis for survival, priorities changed. Family quickly rose to the top of our list, and so began our annual family reunion. Deciding to focus on what was important rather than attractions, we voted to rough it at a place that would allow us to enjoy nature while reveling in our family ties.

Brad and I packed our two cars, a flatbed trailer, and a twenty-foot U-haul full of stuff needed for the three day excursion and prepared to head off into the wild blue yonder to the campsite we'd agreed upon as a meeting point.

"Did you get the air mattresses and the flannel sheets?"

"Yes, dear."

"What about the generator, little TV, portable stereo, and pump?"

"Check, check, check, and check."

"Did you tuck my makeup case and butane curling iron into the drawer of the folding vanity? Oh, and the power cords so the mirror works—"

"That is not a makeup case. It's more like a trunk. I packed it next to the vanity, and the power cords are in the drawer. Are you sure you need all of this?"

"I *absolutely* need all of it. I wouldn't be caught dead in the wilderness without mascara, lipstick, a hot shower, and a phone. You did get the cell phones, didn't you?"

"Yes, dear. Did you get your bathing suit?"

"That's the one thing I can do without. No need to scare the fish, right? They never did anything malicious to me. I think we're ready. Let's go"

We made it twenty-seven miles away from home before noticing we'd forgotten the kids.

After setting up the four-bedroom tent, solar enclosed shower unit, the gas fireplace, and a deck built off the back entrance, we strolled on over to see how Uncle Pete was doing with the kitchen area.

Uncle Pete is the ultimate camper. He's the one everyone wants around in times of famine. Well, him and his kitchen unit. He'd built himself a modern day chuck wagon out of an old truck bed, a few welded posts, and some old sliding doors. When he opened it up, clouds parted and light from heaven encircled his creation, beckoning men within a two-mile radius to come pay homage to this thing of marvel. It made onlookers wonder if anyone had ever seen a stainless steel sink and eighteen burners before.

It took him a matter of a few minutes to unfold, set up, and unpack the unit. When he was done, even I was impressed. Julia Child would be right at home in the wilderness with this portable kitchen.

A moose who'd stopped by to see what the commotion was all about stopped in his tracks and gazed enviously at the back of the wagon. I followed his line of vision to see—holy cow! I hadn't seen that during my quick perusal! I nodded in understanding as I looked at the huge rack full of spices. It alone had more shelf space than Schilling at any major grocery chain. If Julia didn't pounce on that rack, then I was fairly sure the moose would.

Uncle Pete jumped right into cooking a seven course dinner

complete with a three-layer cake for Aunt Emily's fiftieth birthday celebration that night. He looked like Edward Scissorhands as he chopped and diced. He had it *so* under control that those rare few who actually could dodge the flying pans, knives, and vegetables stayed behind, while the rest of the group decided to hike around the nearby lake.

A while later, Tyler came flying back to our humble home away from home carrying a treasure he'd found while hiking. It was a beautiful little clay pot with a scene of a serene sunset over looking a mountain range.

"Where'd you find this, Ty?"

"In the meadow. I almost stepped on it. I can't believe someone would just throw it away." Neither could I. I took the pot from him and looked at it closely. There was a bunch of cotton and grass stuck in it. Odd, I thought as I pulled it out and peered inside.

"Land sakes, Tyler, it's someone's ashes!" I looked at the bottom of the pottery and sure enough, there was a piece of faded tape with barely discernible writing that had a name and a date on it. "It's some guy named Frank. Now be a good boy and *take him back* and we'll gladly kiss his ash goodbye!"

Tyler grinned at me in defiance, grabbed the pot, and ran off to play show-and-tell with Dad, the perpetual jokester. Dad, of course, rather than being the voice of reason, came up with a plan in which Frank would be Auntie Em's surprise guest of honor.

"Dad, we can't present her with a dead guy! Have a little sense."

"I am. Life is too short to take seriously. Just ask Frank here," and with that he hobbled off to find a pillow case and a vine to wrap up Frank's remains in for Auntie Em's celebration later that night.

Now anyone who knows Aunt Emily knows that there are only two things in the world that drive her nuts—being tickled and any-thing dead. Dad simply hadn't been able to resist the urge to have some fun with the situation that had just presented itself.

While the first and second generation women went for a nice drive through the countryside, the third and fourth generations decorated the camp with black balloons, black streamers, and dead (or at the very least, really, really sick looking) flowers. Other than our color scheme, Justin's Grateful Dead t-shirt was the only clue as to what she was in for.

When Auntie Em arrived back at camp, she figured something was up but hadn't a clue as to the extent of our shenanigans. It was probably a good thing, or she would've fainted dead away.

Dad started off with a speech. "Emmie, can we please have you come up? Everyone move back a bit, we want her right about dead center—here." Dad pointed. "We are gathered here today to pay tribute to a brave spirit, who has pioneered this family through the rough times and, quite frankly, who also leads us in most of the fun!" There was a moment of silence followed by a spirited round of applause.

"I'm dead serious here, folks." Dad looked around for emphasis. "Emily, may I be frank with you? You're a woman who's an example to us all when it comes to grace, laughter, and spirituality, and just between you, me, the fence ghost . . . umm . . . I mean post, I hope you're not too gravely disturbed by this loving display of affection. So in the spirit of fun before we all become zombies, let's raise our hot chocolate to Emily, our favorite ghoul—er, ah-hem, excuse me; frog in my throat—gal and let the parade of presents begin!"

"Well, frankly, I'm a little surprised at your lack of long winded-ness. Usually, you kill us with your lengthy speeches." Aunt Emily mimicked the theme in a teasing manner towards my father. She still thought the play on words and decorations had to do with her being over-the-hill. She then warmly accepted his toast by raising her mug and swirling it in arc to everyone and said, "You all are just awful!"

Grandma, with a twinkle in her eye, replied, "You're dead wrong. Now come on over here and bury your backside." She pulled her down into a folding lounge chair that'd been set up by the campfire from where she could open the gifts that were being tossed into her lap.

She was in pretty high spirits until she opened the pillow case with the hastily tied vine. There was a long silence, and her skin turned ashen before she momentarily buried her face in her hands. Garnering her courage, she opened the pillow case again and looked at the little ceramic vase, instinctively knowing what it was. She'd caught wind of the rumors about Tyler's great find but had also heard the planned and well-circulated report that Frank had been returned to his place of rest.

"Thanks, guys, you all sure know how to kill a good time." She laughed and gingerly handed the pillowcase back to Tyler. "Now, what's for dinner?"

"What else, Em, but frankfurters over Pete's Franklin stove!" said Dad.

After everyone's bellies had been sated and a few ghost stories shared around the campfire, Auntie Em yawned. "I'm dead beat. Good rest to you, everyone!" She then headed off to her tent.

The day of our departure, she ran around and gave everyone hugs and kisses while Tyler and Justin returned Frank to the meadow. Brad and I filled a baggie with campfire ashes and placed them in her sunglass case. As I hugged her goodbye, I told her (frankly, speaking of course) that I hoped she'd rest in peace during her long journey home. She laughed, gave me a hug, jumped in her car, and headed on down the canyon road. Ten minutes later, those of us who were left roared with laughter as her scream echoed all the way back up to our campsite.

Later on that year in October, we received a package in the mail. The card said:

> Halloween is almost here.
> So I thought I'd send some holiday cheer.
> It's a friend of mine, who's quite divine.
> He floats around and doesn't make a sound,
> But wants to stay despite a little decay
> With the family I love the most,
> And whose mantle will make the best host.
> Happy Halloween!
> Love, Aunt Emily

"Hey kids! We have company for a few months!"

"Who is it?"

"Someone who doesn't take up much room or eat a lot," I said. I looked into the beer stein at the wadded up bag of ashes. "Frank-in-stein, cute Aunt Em, real cute," I mused.

He stayed . . . but only until Christmas.

Brad and I had received an invitation to attend a party where we were supposed to bring gag gifts. I sent my RSVP and said we'd love to come in the spirit of good will and good cheer! I placed Frank in a ceramic vase and taped some pennies around the mouth of the jar topping it off with a cork. Putting him in a well padded box, I then wrapped it in the most decadent paper I could find, finishing it off with a glorious golden bow. I then fashioned a special tag in the form of some golden bells, attached a type written rhyme, and tied it onto the package.

The couple who got our gift read the card out loud,

> Long ago in Bethlehem, a special child was born.
> This sweet baby we'd call king, and many his name
>   would adore.
> Kings and wise men came a-calling and shepherds
>   with flocks a-following,
> Bringing gifts fit for a king, hence—gold, myrrh and
>   frankincense.
> We share this bounty with our friends and hope this
>   season souls will mend.
> May the holiday spirit be with you,
> Brad and Stacy

"You guys are supposed to bring a gag gift. This is way too beautiful to open."

"Just wait until you hear the rest of the story," I then proceeded to tell them about Frank and our family reunion. She opened the package and looked at the vase with absolute repulsion.

"This is dead wrong," she stoically deadpanned as she crammed the tissue paper back into the box and closed the box flaps. She then turned to her husband and with a mischievous glint in her eye said, "I know! Let's send him to Kent and Jackie in Columbus! She faints whenever anyone says boo, and he dies of laughter at that face she makes when going out for the count."

"I don't know, hon—the guilt would haunt me forever." The rest of the night was filled with enough laughter and one-liners to put any comedy club to shame.

Last I heard, Frank was in Milwaukee. He's been touring the country more than a chain letter. Frankly, I hope he makes it to Vermont. I hear it's beautiful there this time of year.

Life Lesson Number Twenty-five:

Walt Disney once said, "All your dreams come true if you have the courage to pursue them." It's good advice from a guy who succeeded by living most of his life in a fantasy land with a six-foot mouse and a duck who never wore pants.

If I Want to Get Over the Rainbow, Can I Use a Stepstool?

Is there life after kids? Or am I destined to a life containing not much more than fabric pre-treaters for spots where Brad has dribbled strained prunes. Or a dust wand that works temporary wonders on the living room coffee table but can't quite grab the cobwebs from an underused mind. And last but not least, a garden hose that is two feet too short to get to all the dry spots in my front yard but long enough to help me remember a basement watermelon patch and a little tow-headed boy I'm already beginning to miss.

Maison was getting older. Next September he'd be off to school, which meant that he'd eventually come to rely on the outside world for his happiness a lot more than he would me. Even though I felt too young to retire, my sons thought I was older and farther out of their youthful realm than moon rocks. Whether I wanted it to or not, time was marching onward and they were becoming increasingly independent. My future, I sighed, was becoming glaringly obvious. It was one in which I wouldn't be needed as much anymore.

I personally found it heartbreaking that where I had once looked down into sweet cherubic faces, I was now looking into navels that hadn't been thoroughly cleaned in years. I had to face the facts. Either I was shrinking, or they were growing and spreading out quicker than the spurge from our neighbor's weed patch. Being the perpetual optimist, I bought a three-stair step stool just in case.

Things just weren't as clear as they once had been. I strolled back in time to that day I'd had the epiphany, that day at the circus when the little clowns beckoned to me, making me want to join the most distinguished of sororities—the elite club of motherhood. I had to admit, life up to this point had been a wonderful three-ring circus. Let's face it though—I'd been left with nothing more than a trick car Justin wanted to take every chance he could. He'd even begun volunteering for Mom's taxi service, taking Josh to and from hockey practice, and Mitch to his school and scout activities, which much to my dismay, were becoming more plentiful than the box elder bugs that invaded our home every summer.

Maison was even branching out. My panic mode went into over-drive the day he informed me that Buzz Lightyear was a lot more exciting on the 13" TV with a broken color tube in Carter's room than on our 52" superscreen with stereo surround sound. I knew it was just a matter of time before he packed up his watermelon seeds and headed out the door for good.

I'd only see my sons when they needed money, keys, clean laun-dry, or to warn me that friends were coming. If that were the case, then I would also be politely informed that I was to vacate the prem-ises before any one of their teenage set figured out that the children of my loins had been raised in any other way than through osmosis. I was fairly sure they wished on a regular basis that I would become nothing more than a parental spirit touching their hearts and whis-pering inaudible bits of wisdom—being felt but never really seen.

About the time I found myself having conversations with the Downy dispenser and trying to wipe away my counter's wear and tear spots, which had gotten there by wiping them down so much in the first place, I pulled out my step stool and sat down. In the middle of my kitchen, sitting on a stool I wouldn't need for at least another thirty years when I'd actually have experienced skeletal shrinkage, I lamented my situation and decided that I needed a life. I had reached that sweet and sour day when the kids were spending more time away from our home than in it. I got up to unload the dishwasher again.

As I bent down to put a bowl and lid away in their proper spaces organized by size, texture, and color, I sadly realized that since I was the only one unloading the dishwasher, even the Tupperware didn't need my compulsive organizational skills anymore. And if that wasn't enough, the mending basket was empty since I'd helped all the buttons find their rightful tabs. The garage was clean. The video closet was still alphabetized and the wallpaper wasn't being peeled away by curious little fingers every other day. I looked around almost gagging as I realized all of this had happened before I was even old enough to be sporting an estrogen replacement patch!

I sighed heavily with the sadness of someone heading home from their last frontier and closed the dishwasher. I guess it was time for me to gracefully accept defeat before heading out to pasture with my stud, his bald spot, and the hairs growing out of his ears. And the dog. After all, I surmised, I'd need someone to pull my walker along when I'd lost the conviction to keep treading forward. I picked up Sayde's ball and headed to the back door.

"C'mon, old girl. I'll throw a few until arthritis gets the best of me."

She winced as she stretched the kinks out and slowly took to my side. "How 'bout I just rub your back since arthritis has got the best of you today." She yawned and looked at me with gratitude as I opened the door and stepped out into the crisp autumn air. Then it happened.

I stepped on a pile of little metal cars and fell over the dog, landing in a heap and bruising my backside. Something in me snapped. At almost forty, I was way too young to curl up in my casket and slowly wither away. I began to chuckle. I then stepped up my response to an old-fashioned chortle, which eventually erupted into a full-fledged fit of hysterical laughter.

I got up and wiped off my rear end, picked up a car (I think it was a 1983 Ford Thunderbird, but I had to ask Justin for the definitive answer) and flipped it around in my hand. Sayde wagged her stump of a tail while I mused that it had taken an arthritic dog and a toy to find the fortitude to get back up again. I was old enough to watch my sons walk out the door and into their own lives but still young enough to add value to the world by following my dreams. I'd just have to first remember where I'd misplaced them.

That reminded me, I still needed to clean out my craft closet.

Maybe it was time to dig out the old pen and paper again. What did my high school creative writing teacher know anyway? Every good writer knows, or so I've been told, that you just write about what you know. Well, I knew a lot about nothing. I decided to get busy gathering material and honing my craft.

I got my first freelance assignment as a ghost writer for Mitch when he was asked to speak in church on Father's Day.

Other than the fact Brad didn't exactly cherish the way I portrayed fatherhood in a excruciatingly and rather naked sort of way, I thought it went pretty well, especially since Mitch had taken my first draft of rather comical notes instead of the more serious "Ode to Father" Brad and everyone else was expecting.

Writers brainstorm—that's another rumor I've heard—so I brainstormed, hoping to get in the mood to write a strikingly beautiful piece about the relationship between children and their fathers. I started out by breaking down *relationship* into the words *elation* and *ship* and then sewing a verbal connection between the two. Sadly, all that came to mind was "Yada, yada, yada . . ."

I took a different approach.

I was good at lists. I'd done them my whole life. 1. Clean the fridge. 2. Do the ironing . . . but I digress. Back to my list for Father's Day. I wrote at the top of my paper, "Ten Reasons Why Mitch Should Love His Dad," and for the sake of writer's integrity, I put myself in Mitch's shoes and came up with the following:

1. He is a procrastinator. This means that I don't have to mow the lawn for the first six weeks of summer because he

procrastinated getting a spark plug until after everyone else had bought theirs. The Home Depot guy nicely informed us that there isn't another one to be found in North America until well after the fourth of July.

2. He has a sweet tooth. This means that when Mom tries another diet and throws all the good stuff out, I know I can find his hidden stash of Pop Tarts and Hostess cupcakes under the back seat of our Expedition when I have the munchies.

3. He is hard of hearing when the TV is on. This means that when we are down in the basement watching a really good movie and my mom calls down to us that it's time for bed, we don't get in trouble for not coming up right away because he didn't listen to her either.

4. He snores louder than a sonic jet engine when it's amplified. This means that I feel safe at night knowing that no bad guys would dare come near our house for fear of what may be lurking behind the door.

5. He is forgetful. This means that when he forgets Mother's Day, it makes the cards I make for my mom and my grandmothers really stand out as something special.

6. He likes pancakes as much as I do. This means that when I ask Mom if we can have pancakes for breakfast on Saturday and she says no, Dad is down in the kitchen in his underwear and an apron with a spatula in his hand and a stack off 39 blueberry pancakes already done.

7. He is an impulsive buyer. This means that even though he had been laid off from his job, I still get season tickets to the hockey games because the tickets on eBay were too good a deal to pass up.

8. He has a sense of humor. This means that when Mom is yelling at us because we're having a water fight in the house, Dad gets in as much trouble because he's using the sprayer from the sink and drowns her after she just got done cleaning the kitchen.

9. He likes hockey. This means that I don't have to weed the yard until June when the Stanley Cup play-offs are over.

10. And the number one reason why I like my Dad? Because he's always there for me. This means that he helps me when I need

help. He never puts things or possessions before me. He teaches me how to do my best. He teaches me right from wrong and does all of this while also teaching me that I am loved, how to laugh, and how to enjoy life and the blessings I've been given.

I would've liked to have taken credit for that sentimental and touching ending, but Mitch scribbled it in when he needed an ending for his talk that was supposed to be given in twenty minutes. I couldn't help him. I'd fallen asleep on the couch at three in the morning and fatigue was making me run late again. I hadn't realized that he'd scribbled his nostalgic gibberish onto the wrong copy until he was blaring it through a microphone from the pulpit. I did hear some laughter though, and it gave me encouragement. At least, I could possibly succeed as a writer for celebrity roasts.

I began to look at things in a whole new way. My mind became inquisitive as I looked at the world around me and began pondering the deeper mysteries in life like why when I called on my credit card account line, did the automated teller tell me to press nine if I needed the TTY service for the hearing impaired?

And why when I drove up to the drive through ATM at my bank, did they have all the instructions posted in Braille under the transaction screen?

Why did the Wyoming government spend money to put up a sign that says, "Lamont Pop 3 Elev 6622"?

What happens when someone dies, gets married, divorced, or heaven forbid, has triplets? Talk about a population boom. Lamont, Wyoming would suddenly double in size! (A word to the wise at the Barnes and Noble marketing division, I don't see much of a future there. You'd lose money on the cappuccino alone.)

Why did crew neck monogrammed sweaters have to become the high school rage when I was there? For Christmas my sophomore year, I'd been given nine sweaters that my parents had proudly had monogrammed with my initials. Too bad they hadn't thought about the repercussions to their teenaged daughter's sanity after having walked around for three years with SAG written across her chest.

Why do parents always tell their children at age eleven to grow up when they want them to do chores and babysit, yet when the kids are asking for the car keys and wanting to wear high heels and makeup at that same age, they tell them to act their age?

Why did the farmer on Clayton Road, who we passed every Sunday on our way to church, post a big sign out front that said, "For sale, VERY, VERY clean dirt." Even more thought provoking was the idea of who would actually buy it.

I sat down at my laptop to begin. I stared at the blank screen with the blinking curser until I had edema in my ankles and a bad case of carpal tunnel syndrome. I typed, "If there is no beginning, there can be no end!" before booting down and heading out to the mailbox.

It was a good mail day. Three grocery ads, only one bill, and a sample wrapped in a blue box. I pitched the bill into a drawer and sat down to read the ads and open my sample. Rump roasts were on sale. Not a bad price either. Too bad Dad's tush tumor had put a damper on any excitement I might have previously had over a slow simmered rump roast with potatoes. Great hunks of flesh had just about lost all appeal after seeing his surgical pictures with radiation catheters poking out of him like well-placed meat thermometers. Those visuals had pretty much soured my carnivorous taste buds for the next decade.

I turned to the blue box and opened it. Out fell a coupon, a smaller box containing three feminine supplies in pearlesque wrappers, and a scratch and sniff card that smelled like a springtime bouquet. I could think of better samples but, hey, it sure beat stepping on a rusty nail and a tetanus shot.

I decided to go to the bookstore. I always go to the bookstore when I need to relax and escape the drudgery of dealing with extreme brain cramps. Besides, maybe I could find a direction for my life and career while perusing the titles of places I'd like to go.

I picked up the blue box and ran upstairs so I could touch up my makeup and redo my hair. The approaching summer's heat was making the tendrils around my neck uncontrollably frizz out and my mascara and eyeliner were streaming in gothic rivets away from my eyes instead of enhancing them. If I went looking like this, I thought as I looked in the mirror, I'd be caged after having been mistaken for the mythological Medusa.

I reached for my perfume bottle and groaned as it spritzed nothing more than fragrant air. I looked around, grabbed a tampon out of the blue box and rubbed it vigorously on all my pulse points before heading out the door.

I walked into Barnes and Noble and browsed all my favorite sections until I came upon the area where the humor section used to be. I hunted down a clerk.

"May I help you?"

"Yes, where is the humor section now? It used to be right over there. Please don't tell me that there's nothing funny to laugh about anymore. I need a few chuckles here and there especially as the days go on."

"No, it's not gone. We just moved it to a new area. It's now on the same aisle as the war history section. Hey, I love your perfume. It's the perfect summer scent. What is it?"

"Why thank you! It's essence of Playtex . . ."

"What was that again?" she asked as she rummaged through the information counter looking for a pen and a scrap of paper.

"Oh, yes . . . that would be . . . uhhhh . . . essence of pearlesque! Yes, that would be it. It comes in a little blue box. I bet you can get it in most stores. Just ask for the extended wear variety. That way you can smell fresh and clean as a meadow all day long." I smiled and headed off to the war history and humor section.

I think I was definitely on the right track.

Life Lesson Number Twenty-six:

It is what it is.

Onward and Upward

It's back. That insidious villain who has robbed me of memories with so many of the people I have loved. Its name is cancer.

I can barely say the word, let alone acknowledge what it is doing to my dad, but the hoarseness of his voice and the pallor of his skin belie what I am trying to block out—that it has come back with a vengeance and is eating away the organs striving to keep him alive.

He never smoked or drank, and he did all those things that should've helped him beat the odds. But as is the way with life's obstacles in general, cancer is indiscriminate in who it chooses to war with. Never mindful of age, race, gender, or character, cancer will strike without a care of who it destroys in its wake. And so wives are left husbandless, husbands are left without their sweethearts, children become parentless, and parents are left to ache the loss of children who have died before they've had a chance to live.

I know because I've watched it happen time and time again in my life as cancer has claimed yet another victim. Watching this casualty however was proving to be the hardest. They say practice makes perfect but in death, no amount of practice can ever give you a perfect understanding or an ability to handle it perfectly. Quite honestly, it just sucks.

At sixty-one, Dad was becoming a shell of the man who had always been my knight in shining armor, but my eyes, or rather my heart, could only see him for what he'd always be to me—my hero.

His sickness made him even more so because he handled it with grace, dignity, and patience while the rest of us stumbled through moments of not knowing what to say or how to react.

I chose to believe and blocked out any notion whatsoever that he could possibly be beat by this. "He is, after all, invincible," I mentally chanted, not wanting to admit that those thoughts sprang from a small girl's perceptions of always having felt safe in her daddy's arms. He couldn't die. What would the world—more specifically, my world—be without him?

It was easy to think he'd beat it as he managed a strong upper lip while making everyone around him laugh and feel better. It wasn't until much later, as we looked back, that we finally realized he'd long since known it would get the best of him. But he had also been adamant that no one should mourn before he was gone. Wanting to savor every moment left in this life, he'd allowed us to carry our torches burning bright with the oil of hope.

It wasn't for selfish reasons he'd allowed our delusional living—it had been because he'd seen the need for each of us to come to the same conclusion he had but in our own time, through our own means, and when each of us could deal with it the best. He was letting us grow in faith and understanding, not wanting to force terminal realization upon us.

I'm still not sure when he knew though.

It could've been the week he began losing his hair by the fistfuls for a second time. That had been when I'd first seen him at a loss for words, sinking into a bit of melancholy—but not for long. He tackled his hair loss like any other challenge thrown his way, by picking himself up and making the most of what he'd been given. He held a fireside for the local youth and talked to them about adversity.

"Only you can decide how you will handle the challenges placed before you. You can let them beat you, or you can take the upper hand," he admonished.

After explaining his circumstances, he then invited each teenager to come take a swipe at his head with a pair of electric shears. I think there were more tears falling onto his emerging baldness than hairs that were shaved off. I bent over picking up a clump of his dark curls and held them tightly in my fist.

As I looked at his smiling face, laughing and joking with the youth in his neighborhood, I saw strength and knew without a doubt he'd beat it.

Maybe he had known when his doctors asked him if he'd be part of an experimental study. His oncologist had known it was a last-ditch effort and maybe somewhere in his heart he had known also. He signed the paper work, making him the first man in the world to use the new drug, then known as OS1774, in sarcoma cases.

I watched him as he religiously took this new medication and hopefully thought that maybe there was a chance he could beat it.

Maybe he had known that last Christmas as he hobbled around, trying to buy gifts for his family that would convey what they meant to him. He was finally forced to give up, unable to breathe without being tethered to his oxygen and unable to take the pain from being on his feet. He was worn out and wanted simply to spend what little energy he had enjoying his family while listening to the laughter, watching the excitement in the grandkids' eyes, and capturing every miniscule moment.

I watched him from the kitchen as he smiled through a hint of sadness because he was on the sidelines, unable to be involved in this year's Nerf wars. I was beginning to wonder if he could beat it.

In March, he asked me over so he could talk with me and my husband. Could I come soon? I forgot my errands and rushed to his side. Everyone else was there too.

That night as my mom fitfully slept on a bed next to his chair, I stayed awake to watch him, trying to process what these moments meant.

I was losing him and he—my hero—was unable to beat it.

He stirred, sat up and choked a bit, struggling to breathe. While measuring out his morphine, I went back to a conversation I'd had with him fifteen years before. We'd been driving home from Arizona, just the two of us, after having delivered a car to a family member. It was the only time he'd spoken candidly to me about the things which made him human, like his struggles, weaknesses, and fears.

"I've always figured I would die young. Maybe it's history seeping into my thoughts, but I don't think so," he said.

"That's pretty morbid. Are you trying to ruin this drive home?"

He laughed. "No, I'm more just wanting to enjoy every moment and be thankful for the life I've had." He reached over to correct the wheel since I was staring at him with my mouth gaping open. "Keep your eyes on the road, will ya? There's a lake over there, and no matter what, I don't want to go by drowning. I can't think of a worse way."

I snapped back to the present and offered Dad the dropper full of medicine. But before it put him into another deep sleep, I took a few moments during the wee hours of that still night to tell him something I'd wanted to say.

"Daddy, I'm so sorry you have to go this way. Of all the things I wish I could take from you . . . the fluid filling your lungs . . ."

His hand reached out to cover mine. He breathlessly squeezed out the words "Stace, it is . . . what it is. In the eternal scheme of things . . . this life is only . . . about twenty minutes . . . I can do anything . . . for twenty minutes."

I put my head on his lap because I wanted to feel the warmth of him and also to hide my tears and what little strength I had in keeping it together. I finally looked up. "Promise me you'll come back, even if we can't see you, promise me you'll be here for the important events."

"I've never done this before, Stace. I don't know what the rules are . . . I need to find out . . . what they are first." He stopped to catch his breath. "And then I'll figure out which ones can . . . be bent." He smiled and touched my hair.

"Are you afraid, Daddy?"

"Not afraid to go on, just . . . feel . . . cheated for what I have to . . . leave . . . behind. Love . . . you," he barely rasped before drifting off. It was the last time I spoke to him.

He passed away on March 28 with my mother and all six children holding him. My hand was on his chest when his heart beat for the last time.

People die every day. Admittedly, it's a part of the circle of life but that does not necessarily make it easier when someone you love who's been cheated dies all too early. The gross injustice of it all just manages to tick you off and question what kind of God is up there playing with all of our lives anyway.

In a sadistic sort of way, it's nice to know that we're all in it together. Life is tough and it's a pretty sure bet that no one will make it out alive. But when you're grieving alone, and your world has been rocked and forever changed, it's hard to remember that while you feel like you're going through it alone, you're doing it together. That simple fact—through the commonality of the battles we've fought—makes us, if you will, a virtual family of sorts.

I learned something else too. Grief is a must if you've loved someone fiercely.

As I watched my mother ache and weep until she was numb, I realized that even if I could, I wouldn't take away the pain of his death. To do so would also take the love out of her life and that would have been a greater tragedy. And so we lived with the pain and anguish as well as the memories and lessons of his life. At that time, however, I had no way of knowing just how deep my mother's grief and loneliness was.

My father loved the outdoors and reading, but most of all he loved his family, life, and serving his fellowmen, which is why when he began having back troubles and a knot formed in his leg, the imposed limitations just about killed him. Several doctors diagnosed his problem as nerve damage, attributing the knot to muscles that were constricting in his leg as they were being further damaged.

When a doctor finally diagnosed his problem correctly, a mass, known as a nerve sheath sarcoma, had grown to the size of a football, encapsulating his sciatic nerve. By that time, cells had broken off and spread to his lungs.

Even towards the end of his life, service to his fellowmen was foremost in his mind. His thoughts were of a future generation as he signed on to take part in the experimental study. Even though in his heart he'd known it was too late for him, his hope was that the data gathered from his case might enable doctors to make further progress in the fight against the disease.

Until the day he died, he'd been heavily involved in doing whatever he could to promote the good work being done in his own backyard and other facilities and treatment centers around the world.

Four days before Dad died, my brother Devon asked him if he'd known the medicine would never work. Dad replied that he'd known all along that it was too late for him, but what could possibly be learned from his case, would help the next guy down the road. Cancer was his battle, but he hoped to aid efforts to ensure that it wouldn't have to be someone else's.

He understood the toll cancer took on people's lives. He'd lost his father to cancer at sixty-five—a melanoma that hadn't been biopsied for further growth. My mother had lost her father to cancer at age sixty. He'd been one of Southern Utah's down-winders. Out of the ten children in his family, seven of them had died at early ages of cancer. My maternal grandmother had been widowed at fifty-seven. My paternal grandmother at sixty-two. Mom was now a widow at fifty-nine. Our family wasn't ignorant of the evils and possibilities of cancer; we were acutely aware of its effects.

And they did not stop there.

A very short time, three years to be exact, as we were just beginning to heal from Dad's passing, cancer struck again. My mom was sixty-three when she was diagnosed with stomach cancer and also named as one of Southern Utah's down-winders. This time, I was the one to stand by her side having patience, adding strength, and holding onto faith, believing that all would be well.

I remembered when she lost her dad at twenty-nine, and on the day of his funeral, she had cried but told me that she had thanked God for giving her such a wonderful man as a father.

And when she was losing her father-in-law at thirty-seven, I watched as she took on the house, five children, the yard, and the budget so Dad could fly back and forth between Denver and Phoenix, spending what precious time there was left with his father. At grandpa's funeral she shed tears and thanked God that she'd been blessed with another good man who'd raised a fine son—the one she had grown to love more than life itself.

And when Dad developed his persistent limp, she chauffeured him from doctor to doctor in a fervent quest, hoping to find the cause. She had been forced to, once again, face cancer and bravely took my Dad's hand saying, "We'll fight this together."

On the eve of Dad's death, mom wept as she rested her head upon his knee, knowing he was steadily growing closer to taking his last breath. And although for most of her married life she had been afraid to give voice to her darkest trepidations, we children knew that her biggest fear had always been to be left alone. Yet, she lifted her head and whispered so those in the room could barely hear, "I love you, but I can do this. I don't want to see you hurt anymore. Go, my love, go . . ."

Moments later, Dad took his last breath. Mom kissed him gently on the forehead and left the room to make the arrangements.

On the day of his funeral when every cell in my body wanted to scream at the injustice of it all, my Mom put her hand on my shaking arm and said, "I thank God for having such a wonderful man to share my life with," and she sadly but tenderly watched as the love of her life was being put to rest.

Mom's doctors told us that her case was a complex one and quite frankly, that was fitting, since she was a complex woman. Although her emotions were clearly defined, her words often were not. She loved fiercely and fought to keep her family close but sometimes we as children just heard the fight part and not the love behind them.

She said she was never good with words, but she gave amazing talks and loved to learn new and unusual words in the dictionary and engage in word play.

She could cry and laugh at the same time.

She was every bit a lady but was also a tomboy. As a little girl, she ran through fields, played in mud and with snakes, and even once wore her boy cousin's underwear.

She always praised others and marveled at their talents but had a hard time recognizing her own as true gifts and as marvelous works.

She said she couldn't die—she had not found her purpose in life—yet she gave everything to her family and friends.

She sometimes questioned her own faith, yet she had the uncanny ability to teach faith, perseverance, strength, and forgiveness by example through the things she did on a daily basis.

But on the evening of her death, there was no mistake as to her feelings. We wondered why she did not just give up and go. Her body was racked with pain and as much as it was excruciating to let her go, she held on with a fierce determination, proving once and for all that she was indeed more stubborn than any of us had previously known.

Although she had not been responsive for more than twenty-four hours, right before her passing her breathing calmed, her eyes barely opened, and she looked at her children. As testimony to our mother's love and complex ways, tears of joy and anguish ran down her face before we had the opportunity to usher her into Dad's waiting arms.

As I had driven her to and from appointments, I'd had many opportunities to talk with her and understand the true nature of her heart and the tenderness she had for her children, her grandchildren, her other family members, and her friends. And if there was a word that could define those conversations besides love, it was gratitude.

I had also watched many times during the years since Dad's

passing as she'd forlornly gazed at Daddy's picture and harbored insecurities that she couldn't do it as well as he had—couldn't laugh as much, couldn't live as well, or love as perfectly as he did. But every day she faced, she did it as best she could, hoping to make proud those who meant most to her in this life as she found moments to laugh and love perfectly—just like she had taught Daddy to do.

And then I remember the night when she talked one last time of the birds. It was the night she asked me to be the mother bird—she was counting on me to be the heart and glue to our family. She told me to be there for Bethie and do all those things she'd need another woman's touch for. She told me to make sure the boys played nice and that she wanted them all to know that she knew their hearts and that they had made her extremely proud. She then gave me the charge to make sure all feathers were kept unruffled, and when they were, to make sure they did not stay that way.

On the day of her funeral, while all of the family was round saying their good-byes, as the family's new matriarch, I remained strong by remembering her example and thanking God for giving me a mother that had taught me how to be the mother bird. But when everyone had departed and I was left alone with her casket and a lifetime of memories, I crumbled.

I embraced her gleaming wooden coffin and cried until my tears ran freely down the cover and into the cement crypt waiting below. I cried until no more tears would come. I then got up, bent down, and kissed the box that held my mentor, my friend, my mother, and promised to watch over my siblings like a hawk.

Now when I find myself missing my parents, I sit down with a pair of Dad's old wingtips in my lap and Mom's pearls around my neck and envision myself walking in his shoes with her grace, doing as they would've done. Then I get up and go to work, paying homage to them while becoming a better person. In that sense, I keep them alive, and they manage to keep inspiring me by being my heroes and my mentors.

I still don't understand all about their deaths, but I am pretty sure of one thing. Many people on the other side were waiting to greet and embrace them both, welcoming them into their midst. I'm sure their fathers were there. And another, I know, was my daughter.

I'm also pretty sure Frank was there too, and I'd bet that he said something along these lines, "Listen you two, I have a couple of bones to pick with you. You and your family have been pains in my ash for way too long!"

Life Lesson Number Twenty-seven:

Remember no matter how difficult your problems may be, someone will always have one that is a little harder.

A Hard Situation

I have spoken previously of "the curse." You know the one. The curse flung at you with exaggerated flair several times during your growing up years. The one that eradicates you from a normal existence with your offspring, promising embarrassment and stress a thousand times over what you caused your own sweet and estimable mother.

For some the curse is nothing more than the perpetuation of the circle of life, but for most women who have survived motherhood long enough to see their offspring fight at least a few paternal battles, it is something much, much more. It is proof that there is a just God.

It's a fact that reality will smack most of us in the face at least a few harsh times and if it doesn't, the curse will surely get more than a few sound whompings in. The unfortunate turn of events happens when good luck vanishes, seeing the face of a child tormentor, and allows the curse to rear its ugly head, biting you hard on the backside.

What makes the curse so viable is that mothers universally are a pretty gullible bunch. As a general populous, we will swoon at the sight of a sliver in a three-year-old's finger that was obtained while climbing what heretofore seemed like a hapless tree before calling an attorney to file suit against the National Arbor Association. Never mind that said youngster had climbed twenty feet up the tree while you were chatting on the phone. Thus this ability to be suckered is the hook allowing us to be reeled in as the curse is made into your mother's fulfilled and savored prophecy.

Such was my fortune when Mitch called while I was out running errands to say that Maison had been crying for the better part of an hour and was now to the point of hysteria. I dashed home and scooped him up into my arms, trying to locate the area of his discomfort. He squirmed in agony pulling at his diaper area, tears streaming down his face. Something obviously had to be done.

I rushed him into the ER and after a twenty-second wait, turned venomously on the admitting nurse. "Where's the doctor?"

"We'll be right with you, Mrs. Anderson. Oh, by the way, how is Josh? We haven't seen him in a while. He is still alive, isn't he?"

"What? Oh, . . . yes, he's alive. It's me that should be dead after raising a kid like him," I quipped.

After watching what looked like a prepubescent in a white lab coat pluck a folder from the patient chart cubby hole and listening to another one of Maison's choking sobs, I asked again, "Where'd you say that doctor was? Is he even out of medical school yet or is he back practicing coloring in the lines? Could you possibly move quicker than a napping sloth and get someone out here who has a legitimate diploma and take care of my son *who is obviously in a lot of pain!*"

The nurse looked at me with pursed lips and then turned, whistling down the hall and catching the attention of the triage nurse. "Tell Dr. McKenzie to rush it. The Anderson mother is starting to freak, and I doubt the good doc wants to deal with her child's ailment while his mom sings into her stethoscope while on Valium again."

I glared at her and stated in a hushed tone, "I'll have you know that I was just providing mood music since the tunes on your PA system are about as soothing as nails across a chalkboard."

Back in the examining room, Dr. McKenzie managed to unfold my son from a fetal position and console him to the point of whimpering rather than outright screaming.

"Tell me where it hurts, sweetie, so I know how to help you." He pointed to his diaper area. "Okay, we're going to take a peek so we can see if there is any infection or obvious irritation," she said, while gently undoing the Velcro tabs to see what was causing my son so much pain. Her eyes widened in disbelief as she stared at his groin area before turning towards the door in an effort to gain her composure.

I looked at her and then back to my son before scampering over to pull back his diaper's edge, wanting to see the hideous disorder that had so badly shocked the doctor. I took one look and turned purple with mortification.

Brad peering over my shoulder, looked smug as a pirate who'd just found the buried wealth of the Spanish Armada, and quickly laid claim, "Yup . . . that's my boy!"

I was not as enthused. "And what do I do with that?" I asked the doctor. She turned back giggling.

"It happens to a lot of youngsters as their curiosity is aroused . . . sorry, didn't mean . . . ," she spat out, suppressing her guffaws. "Put him in a cool bath with tub toys to peak his inter . . . I mean, get his mind off things, you get the point. Whoops . . . uh, I'm just going to shut my mouth and let you get him dressed. As for you, little guy," she cradled his chin in her hand looking into his eyes, "next time, let's not make things so hard for Mom and Dad." She chuckled and disappeared as I calculated how I could get out of the front door while avoiding the admitting nurse and all other hospital personnel.

Brad merely high-fived our son and adjusted the cool wet washrag, which was quickly bringing relief.

My sister called me on my cell phone. "I heard what happened," she said, laughing.

"How'd you hear?"

"Mitch called to update me. I must say, I bet Mom is rolling over in her grave, laughing that one of your children has wreaked justice for all the stuff you put her through."

I just smiled and sighed before saying, "Yeah, well . . . whatever small crisis I put her through just remember . . . I have now dealt with something bigger and a lot harder than she ever had to deal with!"

Looking back on things (embarrassment aside), had that been the end of it, I would've been ever so grateful. But as is the way of things, life with its accompanying problems and victories are built and traversed one step at a time. It's a good thing, otherwise we'd all be voluntarily admitting ourselves into the funny farm. I'm thoroughly convinced that life altering change happening too quickly on a regular basis is the recipe, for me anyway, for a scrambled psyche with a side of nervously chewed fingernails.

What had started out as an awkward situation turned into a long drawn out ordeal, which eventually landed us in the hematology/oncology department at the children's hospital. Other than the frequent trips to the doctor's office for suspected bladder infections, there had been no other symptoms—that was until his kindergarten exam.

His urinalysis came back with significant traces of blood. That in itself was not much to worry about, but when he received his immunization shot, the three inch pool of blood left on the paper liner caused quite a bit more concern. A few more tests were run before the doctor returned asking me a few rather pointed questions.

"Has he had bleeding problems before?" asked the doctor.

I scrutinized his face as he kept his eyes glued to the chart. "A few bloody noses that seem to start with no provocation at all."

"You mean he doesn't pick at it or rub it hard, making it bleed . . ."

"Um, yes. Some happen in the middle of the night or while he's just sitting there watching TV."

"Has his behavior or eating habits changed?"

Well, he's seemed kind of tired, not much energy as of late, and he tires out really quickly when his friend Carter comes to play. He's never been a big eater."

The doctor scribbled quickly on a pad and handed me a few sheets. "I want you to head over to the hospital and have some blood tests done as soon as possible."

"What's wrong with my son?" I whispered, knowing in my heart what these tests were for. I couldn't do it again and not with one of my sons.

"Don't worry. We're just ruling out some things." He bid me a good day and backed out the door.

Grabbing my pieces of notepaper with a bit more force than I consciously intended and peering out the door, I watched him conference with another doctor in the practice. The second doctor looked at my son's charts and picked up a reference guide on pediatric oncology.

I closed the door and slid down the back into a fetal position on the floor, not realizing I'd scrunched the note paper and dropped them as my hands came to my face. Mitch put his hand on my shoulder and asked what was wrong. I could see his mouth moving, but I could not for the life of me hear a word he said. Time froze and every motion, word, and breath seemed to play out like a scene in slow motion.

I'm not sure how I made it to the car or drove to the hospital. Thanks to Mitch's intuitiveness, Brad was there to meet me as I walked, still in a daze, into his outstretched arm. Maison had already jumped up onto his daddy's other arm, perched like a colorful parrot in his new Hawaiian print shirt.

Later that night I sat in the quiet darkness of my living room and wept. Could a loving God be so cruel as to put me through this yet again?

Although God didn't spare me the agonizing ups and downs of hope and reality through numerous tests, waiting, more tests, hospital visits, more doctors and surgery, He did give me strength. At least I'm pretty sure it had been divine intervention because no human feat could've gotten me through those months with my sanity intact.

Although Maison's blood work and tests somehow miraculously came back negative for leukemia, every test thereafter came back pointing to something darker and more sinister than simple complications. Even though I knew what the dark circles under his eyes and the suspicious images on his scans could mean, I still prayed for another miracle and was not beneath begging or bartering for my son's life. I shamelessly made a habit of it every moment I had alone, or wasn't talking aloud, chanting my requests and bargains.

Nowhere was I more adamant that my prayers be heard than in the waiting room while Maison was undergoing exploratory surgery to biopsy the lesions and masses found within his little body. If it were possible to will an outcome, I admittedly was doing everything in my power to make that happen.

When the doctor finally entered the room still dressed in green scrubs with droplets of blood smudged at the edge of his waist, I held my breath, waiting for the answer I so desperately wanted to hear.

"It's the strangest thing. I could see several areas where there had been lesions but nothing was left but scar tissue where they had healed. I checked the area where we'd seen the two largest spots on his scans, but examination found nothing to indicate anything other than a boy who's been completely healed. I couldn't find any signs of cancer whatsoever."

I sunk back into my chair, tears quickly filling my eyes and scarcely audible to anyone beyond my circle of friends and family, mouthed the words into cupped hands, "Thank you, thank you, thank you," to the doctor as well as to my Heavenly Father.

It was nice to finally know rather than to merely hope that prayers are answered and miracles still do happen in a very uncertain world.

Life Lesson Number Twenty-eight:

❦

Is this my pot of gold or life's form of crime and punishment? The answer is yes, and honestly, life couldn't be any richer!

So This Is Nirvana?

Life is a funny thing. Really. I want my tombstone proudly declaring that I died of laughter choking on a good joke.

I once heard a joke about a pessimist and an optimist. A doctor wanted to see if these tendencies were inbred or learned—you know the whole nature versus nurture debate. Anyway, the doctor filled two rooms. One room he filled with every toy a child could ever want and the other he filled with nothing more than heaps and heaps of cow dung. He then put the optimistic child into the room with all the manure and the pessimistic child into the room with all the toys. He observed them for twenty-four hours and noted that the child in the toy room sat in the middle of the room with his arms and legs crossed for the entire day while the child in the other room dug and played like there was no tomorrow with a smile on his face. After the observatory period, the doctor then sat down to conference with each of them.

"Why, when you had all of these wonderful toys at your disposal, did you not pick one up to play with or even look at?" he quizzed the first child.

"Well, doc," the pessimistic child replied, "every toy in there is made with several parts and types of materials. The way I see it, they are nothing more than a recipe for disaster. I'd just end up getting hurt, so I decided to save myself the heartache, and my mom and dad the medical bills, and not touch or play with anything."

"I see," said the doctor. He then turned to the other child and asked, "Why did you then find happiness when you were handed nothing more than a huge pile of cow pies?"

"I just figured," the child said, grinning, "that in a room filled with that much manure, there had to be a pony in there somewhere. I'd just have to keep digging until I found it." And with that, the child jumped up and ran back to his room, leaving the bewildered doctor wondering if his own life was filled with the prospect of ponies or piles of toxic . . .

Personally, I'd like to think that my own life has been filled with both—piles of pony pellets that I learned to make into a room full of joys, good times, laughter, tears, memories, and, well, a good life.

The torch was slowly being passed. It had begun the day I decided to be a mom because to be a good mom, you have to work yourself out of a job. The goal is to raise children that are a benefit to society rather than finding their niche through placement on America's most wanted list. A good parent's single focus is to raise children in such a way that, like the birds, they can fly into the expanse of this great place we call our world and take the torch you so begrudgingly, yet pridefully give, along with the car keys and your last twenty-dollar bill.

Raising my sons has been a lot like the cedar hope chest I kept in my room as I was growing up. I filled it with every little trinket and memento that I thought would add glitz and happiness to a future I had not yet embarked upon. At the same time—deep down in the hidden caverns of a tenuous heart—there was a huge part of me that really just wanted to keep the chest safe in my room where I knew we'd be sheltered from a big, scary world. I often wondered what my parents had thought when they had given me the heirloom for my seventeenth birthday. Had it been a ticket to freedom or a safety box?

The bells had barely chimed three o'clock when the door crashed open with an accompanying chorus of "What's there to eat?"

"You know, guys, if you leave that fridge open much longer while you stare at its contents in this heat, something just might grow large enough to step on out and have you for a snack."

Twenty minutes and at least four hundred kilowatts later, they decided on instant fruit drink mix and peanut butter and honey sandwiches, all of which came out of the cupboard. They descended on the food and drink like vultures, leaving just as quickly when the bones I called dirty dishes were the only things left.

"Mom!" Josh hollered from the garage door. "Will you come play street hockey with me?" I looked at the thermometer outside the kitchen window and saw its mercury was peaking at a balmy 99 degrees. Boy, Indian summer had sure hit with a vengeance this year. I yelled back before turning on the dishwasher.

"Is your homework done?"

"No, but I don't have very much. I can do it really quick."

"What is still left to do?"

"A couple of signatures, a math page and a little bit of reading."

The temperature rose another degree. "How many problems, on the math page?"

"Seven."

"How much reading?"

"Ehtyfopgs"

"What? Speak up, you're mumbling." I wiped the sweat dripping down the side of my face.

"Okay, okay. Eighty-four pages but it's only three chapters." Yes! Saved by homework again!

About 9:00 that night, after homework and chores were done, Josh came into my room as I was taking off my shoes to rub my swollen feet. "Mom, after you sign these, will you please go out and play street hockey with me for a bit?"

I looked at my son, sighed, and put my shoe back on. I donned his goalie equipment and posted up in the net, looking like the

NHL's version of the Pillsbury Dough Boy, while he pelted me with balls and pucks. I saved most of them. It was easy since with all that gear on, my hips were wider than the front of the net.

When I really got into the game and danced around in a circle clapping my knees and singing, "Who's your Momma? Who's your Momma? Momma got game! Yeah, woo-woo! Momma got game!" the little bugger called in for reinforcements. My other three sons as well as half the neighborhood showed up to take me down a peg or two . . . or eighty.

I gulped and went back to the crease.

I sashayed, sweated, and blocked until I was on the verge of a diabetic coma. When the game was done, I high-fived all the kids before they headed for home. I was left, at least for now, with just my four and Carter.

"Hey, Mom, you did okay."

"She should've. She fills the net like a bulldozer in front of a lunchbox. Just kidding, Mom. You did pretty good for an old broad." Mitch grinned and slapped me on the back.

Maison and his friend added their approval by whacking each one of my shins and giggling before they ran off to play tag. I took off the helmet and bent over to rub what was invariably going to be a couple of nasty bruises. That's when Josh, in his best Arnold Schwarzenegger voice from the back of the driveway, said, "How abowt one mohr fohr the Joshinator," and pegged me between the eyes with a wicked slap shot.

I think the net broke my fall backwards. Either that or it catapulted me into an ungracious heap to the left side of the driveway. When I came to, I noted that I had Josh's leg pad propped under my head and four boys laying next to me on the edge of the grass, staring up at the stars. Keeping my mouth shut, I subtly looked at the men emerging from behind each of their young faces and cherished this moment under the September sky.

"Where do you think stars come from? They kinda do look like diamonds in the sky, you know like that song says," Josh said to no one in particular.

173

"They're heavenly medals given to angels who show valor in the line of duty," I thoughtfully surrendered.

"Hey, you're awake! I was beginning to worry that we'd have to make breakfast on our own tomorrow."

"Yeah, well, you can't keep a good woman down." I smiled at the realization that I wasn't quite over the crest of motherhood yet.

Josh helped me up and apologized for my swelling nose and blackening eyes. As I reached my feet, he placed his arms around me and said, "I love you, Mom. Thanks for the most excellent hockey moment ever!"

He grabbed my hand as we all headed towards the house. I ushered them on in as I stopped to pick up the random balls lying around and put the net back in its place in the shed. I wiped a bit of blood off the crossbar and smiled. Who would've thought that four boys, a swollen nose, two black eyes, a leg pad, a black sky with thousands of stars, and the most excellent hockey moment ever could've spelled out a middle-aged, overweight female's perfect definition of nirvana?

Certainly not me, but I must admit that I was glad fate and a decision long ago had given me this moment to hold onto for the rest of my life.

Epilogue

If there is one thing I've learned and that I want to reiterate, it is that life is all about perspectives.

Case and point—my sons had finally grown big enough so that they not only could help their paternal grandfather with his yard work, but were also welcomed as additions to his repertoire of trusty garden tools. One of those tools, and the one he was most proud of, was his old fashioned reel lawn mower. He extolled to my sons the virtues of the blades of reel lawn mowers which made them, in his opinion, superior to other mowers.

He was downright giddy as he watched Justin take the mower in hand and started up and down the lawn, mowing in perfect diagonal rows. He directed and conversed over the roar of the motor as it turned the reels over and over, slicing and dicing unwitting blades of grass. My father-in-law then pantomimed the delightful and sophisticated feel of handling a reel lawn mower with a grin on his face.

Justin, meanwhile, just looked at his grandfather and nodded every once and a while and semi-grinned at him while giving him that "Yeah, yeah, Grandpa. This is great, whatever you say, Grandpa" look. After the job was done, my father-in-law slapped him on the shoulder and then caressed the worn handles on the lawn mower.

"Yep, son, there aren't many more reel lawn mowers out there now days and it's a shame. Nothing cuts grass more sharply and cleaner than one of these babies."

Justin nodded, hugged his grandfather, and got in the car rather vexed. "What's the matter, son?" I asked.

"I'm really worried about Grandpa."

"How come?"

"Well, he kept going on and on about his lawn mower like it was the greatest thing in the world. I didn't have the heart to tell him that millions of people around the world have real lawn mowers. They sell them at Sears for cryin' out loud. I mean it's not like the grass fairy cuts everyone else's grass but his and even if she did, he oughta be smoked that he was the only one left out!"

Yep, perspective.

Perspective is why if Brad ever passes on to the great beyond, I am going to marry a sumo wrestler named Tiny, so my thighs look anorexic compared to his and diets won't matter anymore.

I will converse with people like Paris Hilton, so at least in my own mind, the likelihood that my IQ could place me in the upper one-eighth of Mensa's elite is not only a real, but an assured possibility.

It means that the next time I take the cub scouts to day camp and they easily wiggle their little behinds through tractor tires like those I used to easily sit in that are now smaller than the girth of my hips, I am going to realize that back then, my world was just out of perspective and that I was really just living in a delusional reality.

It means that as my children get older and think they are leaving me in the dust along with my rocker, it's time to rock their world and put wheels on the chair and wings on my shoes and race along with them . . . until my cataracts get so bad I can't see where I'm going anymore. And even then—if by spirit only—I will still be the same feisty young gal I've always been, teaching them how to be decent human beings. But until then, there's still a lot of living to do.

In celebration of our twenty-third anniversary, Brad and I took the family to the circus. While there, I couldn't help but zoom back to a former wrinkle in time and remember the teenager surrounded by clowns, a slightly pudgy balding Master of Ceremonies, and three amazing rings of activity. Looking around through the eyes of someone who was still enjoying the ride, my chest swelled with gratitude for almost a quarter of a decade of learning that had given me enough perspective to remain an avid fan of this life's journey. There were a few more crinkles in my face and more than an adequate number of rings around my middle, but everything else was still pretty much like I remembered it.

Right at that moment, an elephant stopped in front of our second row seats and let out a whopper of flatulence before emptying his bowels. I grimaced as Josh jumped out of his seat for a better look.

"*Wow*! Did you look at the bum hole on that one? I bet he eats enough roughage to lay bricks all the way across the Atlantic!"

Some things, fortunately, no matter how much one prays, will never change.

About the Author

Stacy Gooch-Anderson moved often during her growing up years, living in Phoenix, Los Angeles, Chicago, Denver, St. Louis, and finally ending up in Salt Lake City, where she currently resides with her husband and four sons. She is the oldest of six children.

She attended the University of Utah before turning her focus to raising her family. She never abandoned her love of writing, however, and later returned to her roots as a journalist and won several awards through the Society of Professional Journalists for her feature writing and investigative skills.

She began her public speaking career at age eighteen when she was asked to speak at an event with a local TV personality and a nationally renown author. It was then that she found her voice, and her ability to tell stories and draw visual analogies that uplifted and inspired others.

She is currently a corporate trainer for new writers at her company and spends her extra time publicly speaking, teaching, writing, and marketing her books. Her first book and national debut was *The Santa Letters*. She is currently working on its companion book, *The Inmate Letters*. She is also a crime victim's advocate through her local police department, acts as a voice for children, and raises money and awareness for cancer research.

She enjoys reading, learning, anything creative, and soaking in the sunshine with her friends and family. She readily admits however, that her greatest source of joy and pride is her husband and four sons, who even on dark cloudy days bring extraordinarily bright rays of sunshine into her life.